I Promised Not to Tell

Raising a transgender child

Written by Mom

I Promised Not to Tell

Raising a transgender child

Written by Mom

Published by Cheryl B. Evans - Ontario, Canada

www.writtenbymom.ca

First Published in 2016

Hardcover ISBN: 978-0-9951807-0-3

Paperback ISBN: 978-0-9951807-1-0

eBook mobi format ISBN: 978-0-9951807-3-4

eBook epub format ISBN: 978-0-9951807-2-7

Library and Archives Canada Cataloguing in Publication

This is a work of nonfiction.

Names have been changed to protect the family's privacy.

First Edition - Revised August 2020

Other books by Cheryl B. Evans include:

What Does God Think? Transgender People and The Bible

Wonderfully and Purposely Made: I Am Enough

My Parenting Journey with an LGBTQ+ Child: A Journal

My Parenting Journey with a Transgender Child: A Journal

I Love You Unconditionally: A Journal for LGBTQ Children & Teens

Dedication

I dedicate this book to my two wonderful children. You inspire me and make me want to be a better person. Being your mom has brought me so much joy, even during the challenging times, for you are two of the finest human beings I have ever met and I'm blessed to have you call me Mom. I love you. xoxo

Contents

I Promised Not to Tell

Raising a transgender child

Written by Mom

Introduction

Imagine that you have just had a beautiful, healthy baby. As your baby is being handed to you for the first time, you see her, your perfect baby girl. Taking her tiny hand in yours, you marvel at how small and perfect she is. You take her in your arms and gently kiss her on the forehead as joyful tears fill your eyes. You have waited nine long months to meet your little one, and you are overjoyed that she is finally here. You have taken great care to choose a name for your daughter. Softly speaking her name to her for the first time, you feel an immediate bond.

You simply adore her.

Over the coming weeks and months you clothe her, feed her, bathe her, talk to her and embrace her in every way possible. Your heart is full of love for your daughter and you begin to envision the remarkable life that lies ahead of her. As you hold her close in your arms and look down at those perfect little fingers and toes, her magnificent little face, her eyes filled with wonder and you ask yourself, "What will she do when she grows up?" "What will she look like?" "Will she marry and have children of her own?" There are so many possibilities. Images begin to form in your mind as you envision the life she may have one day, but none of them, not a single vision, prepares you for what is to come. Imagine the unanticipated realization that hits you when you discover, that your daughter, isn't your daughter after all. What you are about to read is our family's true story about discovering the son we never knew we had.

When I initially began to write this, I did so without the intention of it ever being published. I thought of my writing as my own very private, personal, therapy sessions.

This allowed me to put my thoughts down on paper without the fear of ridicule or judgement. I allowed myself to be vulnerable and speak honestly from my heart; often shedding tears as I wrote.

Our family's journey was not always an easy one. The emotional highs and lows I experienced were exhausting. It was like being trapped on a rollercoaster, feeling fearful and elated all at the same time. Wishing it would slow down, even for a minute, so I could catch my breath. Putting my many thoughts and feelings down on paper helped me come to terms with what was happening. There was so much to learn, to acknowledge and to understand. This whole story, which I documented over the course of almost three years, has brought me from ignorance to acceptance.

My family, specifically my husband and two children, mean everything to me. There is nothing I wouldn't do for them. I have learned a lot about myself and each one of them during the time it has taken for this story to unfold. Most importantly, I learned that love, patience and time really do heal.

Along this journey, I became enlightened to the hardships that many transgender people face, some at the hands of complete strangers and some at the hands of their own families. Our society often seems a naïve and cruel place when it comes to the acceptance and treatment of transgender people. It was the knowledge of the existence of these things that got me thinking about sharing our story with the world. Once I thought about this story as one that might actually become published, I began to write about some of the broader issues. I do not want to believe bigotry, hatred and discrimination will win out, but I realize that without stories like ours being told, we can't expect others to understand.

The main problem, as I see it, is the lack of understanding of what it really means to be a transgender person. The more stories that get shared the more I hope we, as a society, can become more understanding, more compassionate and more accepting. If sharing this deeply personal story can make a difference, even for one person or one family, then sharing it will have been worth it. If this story can help to change some of society's negative views towards the transgender community, then I am grateful I found the courage to write it. If this story is able to touch your heart and leave even a small impression on your soul it will have been worth it. If after reading this book, you feel you have gained a better understanding of what it means to be a transgender person then this book has fulfilled its purpose.

Our real names have been changed throughout the book. By doing so, it gave me a way to share our family's story with you and still honour the promise I made to my son when "I promised not to tell." Now, I give you, our story…

Sincerely,

Cheryl B. Evans

PART ONE

Ignorance is Bliss

CHAPTER 1

Two Beautiful Daughters

From the time I was a little girl, I knew I wanted to be a mom. I was twenty six when my first baby was born, a beautiful healthy baby girl. We named her Mariah. When Mariah was on the way I made a commitment to myself that I would do whatever I needed to do, to be able to stay home with her. When my maternity leave was finished, I resigned from my job to make that a reality. Leaving the corporate world behind in favour of becoming a stay at home mom is a decision I have never regretted.

My husband, Jim was wonderfully supportive and worked hard to support our family and make my dream of staying home possible. Looking back, I realize how truly blessed I was to be able to stay home with Mariah. I will always cherish the memories I have from the early years when it was just her and I most of the time. She was a wonderfully bright, very loving, happy little girl and I loved being her mom more than anything in the world.

We took daily walks, often to the park, discovering the outdoors and enjoying the fresh air. We would read every day, something I started doing with her before she was even born. There were the regular nap time and night time stories, but we would always find time to squeeze in extra story time throughout the day. I think we read 'Goodnight Moon' and 'Forever Your Baby I'll Be' a thousand times each. Well, maybe not a thousand times, but often, so very often.

There was always lots of laughing and playing and, when she became a little older, we enjoyed baking together. I scheduled regular play dates with other children her age and kept this going until she entered pre-school and beyond. Mariah may not remember the early years like I do, but I know in my heart they have helped to shape her into the beautiful person she is today.

It was almost four years later before my husband Jim and I were ready to welcome our second child into the world. On one cold winter morning, Mariah's little sister Jordan made her appearance and was absolutely perfect from head to toe. We were blessed with another healthy baby girl. Our first born was thrilled to be a big sister, and she was a great one! She helped me every step of the way, just like a little mommy herself. I was so proud of Mariah. She was a great big sister!

Jordan was a very happy baby. She always awoke in the mornings with a great big grin on her face and was excited to greet the day. She rarely fussed and was content to play on her own or with her sister. The two of them got along very well right from the start. I kept waiting for the sibling rivalry to start, but it never came. They were just two happy little girls.

There were of course times when Mariah would playfully try to hoard mine and Jim's attention, always wanting to be in front of the camera. Who could blame her? She was an only child for the first four years of her life. Mariah may have had some times of jealously sharing the limelight with a younger sibling but she was still a better big sister than I could have ever hoped for. The truth is Mariah was a handful at times but she was very well mannered. In fact, whenever we were out somewhere, people would always comment on just how well behaved she was. Mariah just had a ton of energy and some days I found it hard to keep up with her. Mind you, that didn't stop me from enjoying every minute we had together.

As a little girl, Mariah was shy and slow to take to strangers. Jordan seemed self assured and confident and easily approached people, even people she'd never met before. At home they were almost the opposite. Mariah was the more bubbly of the two and fluttered around the house like a busy little bee. She exuded bountiful energy often skipping and singing as she went. With her favourite dolls always close at hand. Where Jordan, on the other hand, was often seen entertaining herself, quietly playing with her toys or drawing a picture. Then there were the times I loved to witness the most. Mariah and Jordan happily playing together, whether it was playing hide n seek, or just running around in the yard. Watching them play and listening to them laugh; those were the sweetest moments for me.

I could not have been happier. I was married to my best friend, a man I admired and respected, and still do. We had two beautiful daughters who quite literally lit up my world and, together, we were the traditional family I had always wanted. Everything seemed as it should be.

It wasn't long however before Jim and I began to notice that our two daughters were even more different than we first realized. Our first born, Mariah, loved pink and purple, Barbie dolls, baking cookies, playing dress up, and doing all the other typical little girl things. While her younger sister Jordan loved blue, baseball caps, toy cars and would only agree to play Barbie dolls with her sister if she could be Ken. Jordan gravitated to little boys as she grew a little older. In fact, her best friends were always boys. They would skateboard, play ball, army, and build forts. She even wanted to collect and trade playing cards (remember Yu-Gi-Oh?) and so, she did. None of these were things her older sister wished to partake in.

While our older daughter Mariah had a love for dance and took up many different types of dance lessons, her younger sister Jordan did not share this love. When Jordan was old enough we enrolled her in dance with Mariah but she hated it. She cried saying she wanted to quit after the first class. Jordan wanted to have no part of dance and insistently begged us to enrol her in karate and basketball. We supported their uniqueness and happily accommodated them by enrolling them in these different extracurricular activities. Each of them flourished in the classes they had chosen for themselves. We were proud parents, attending and watching every class we could.

There was a time when Jordan was about three years old and had made up this little song that went something like this: "Just call me Jake, yep Jake, that's my name, that's my name. My name is Jake and I have big kid underwear in my drawer, YA!" We would laugh so hard. It was like a celebration telling whoever would listen that potty training was complete and like the commercial says "I'm a Big Kid Now". We never thought anything of it at the time. It was just a silly little song our tomboy daughter would sing while up on top of a little red stool in the middle of our family room with a pretend microphone in hand.

Jordan would share her play name "Jake" with others too, like my cousin Leanne. While I have several cousins there are none I am closer to than Leanne. Leanne and I have been close since we were little girls and I think of her like a sister. She spent a great deal of time at our house when my children were young and, in many ways, was like a second mother to them. Leanne would tell me how she thought it was funny how Jordan referred to herself as Jake when she was playing. She said Jordan had even asked her to call her Jake rather than Jordan on occasion. We had no idea where that name came from. We didn't even know anyone named Jake. Perhaps it was the name of a character on one of the cartoons shows Jordan and Mariah watched. I honestly have no idea.

Leanne was an important part of our lives and both Mariah and Jordan developed strong bonds with her. Aside from my parents, there was no one Jim and I trusted our children with more than Leanne. When Mariah was seven and Jordan was three, Leanne had a special gift idea she thought my kids could surprise me with. It was quite common for her to take the girls out for a few hours or even a full day so pulling off this little coup was not difficult. I'm not sure how the girls kept the secret from me as to where Leanne had taken them that day, but they did. They never gave me so much as a hint to where they had gone or what they had been up to. Leanne had taken them to have professional glamour pictures taken. She had the pictures specially framed and the kids surprised me with them on Christmas morning. They turned out beautifully and I loved them. There were some of just Mariah, some of just Jordan and a couple of the two together. In addition to the pictures I also received one more surprise that Christmas. It was a very interesting story about all the drama that had ensued in order to capture those wonderful pictures for me.

Apparently, once at the salon, Jordan began to strongly protest the whole idea. Mariah thought that this glam day was going to be fun and exciting but Jordan just wanted to run for the door. Leanne told me how Jordan cried, kicked and screamed while they tried to curl her hair and pretty her up. There was supposedly a ridiculous amount of distracting, joking around, and tickling necessary just to get Jordan to crack a smile or let out a little laugh. Of course, this also involved a dress. It was all in the name of doing something nice for "Mom".

In the end, they got their pictures but the whole fiasco, I was told, was exhausting. Even though the pictures showed Jordan laughing and smiling it was in no way a pleasant experience for her, and guess what? Under the dress, seen in the pictures, Jordan still had on her blue jeans which she insisted were not coming off. Even at three years of age she was negotiating and compromising.

The moment the photos were taken, Jordan was pulling and tearing that dress off. Mariah, I am sure, if they had allowed it, would have taken her dress home with her. The glam day experience for Mariah was very enjoyable. She was my little princess after all. Perhaps having to witness Jordan acting out dampened her overall experience, but knowing Mariah, she was likely doing her best to encourage Jordan to cooperate.

The following summer, when Jordan was four, she began resisting wearing a girl's bathing suit. Rather than have her miss out on learning to swim, I gave in and allowed her to wear a t-shirt and bathing trunks when swimming. One afternoon while camping I took the girls to the campground's public pool for a swim. At the pool there was only the three of us and one other woman with her young son. He looked to be about two years of age.

As soon as Jordan saw this little boy in the pool without a

shirt on, the argument began between me and Jordan. Jordan wanted to go shirtless too. Trying to explain why that was not okay with my young daughter, Jordan began to cry and asked to leave. Looking at the bigger picture, I rationalized with myself about how it was not the end of the world for a four year old girl to go without a shirt. If that's what it took to get Jordan in the pool, fine. Mariah was already wading into the water and looking forward to her time in the pool and asking her to leave now seemed very unfair. I relented and Jordan happily jumped into the water without a t-shirt.

For the next hour my kids had a great time jumping, swimming and splashing around and because there were only two other people in the pool, it was almost like having the place to ourselves. When it came time to leave I said out loud "okay girls, time to go" and the other woman in the pool shot me a strange look. As I was wrapping the kids up in their towels, she looked at me and said "Did you just say girls, time to go?" I said "yes" and then thought nothing more of it. A few hours later, I heard that she had gone to the campground office and made a complaint about how I had allowed one of my daughters to swim without a shirt on. It got back to me that I would not be allowed to take my children to the pool again unless they were both dressed appropriately. Really, people, she is only four!

Jim and I were not one to tell our children they MUST do this or that, and we allowed them to explore their different interests and appreciated them as individuals. I will admit though, we were surprised at just how different our girls were. It still amazes me to this day how multiple children can be raised in the same home, by the same parents, in the same conditions and yet be so completely different (a discussion for another time). The wonderful thing in our family was that our daughters, despite their many differences, were very close. They got along extremely well; perhaps this was because of their differences. After all, there was never any fighting over clothes, toys or friends. Somehow it worked. While it wasn't what we expected having two girls, it is what we got and together, we were a family; a happy family.

During those early years, the biggest challenge for our youngest daughter Jordan began to present itself. She started to question why she was a girl when she was so different from her sister. I remember her asking me as I tucked her into bed one night (I think she was about four at the time) "Mommy, why did God make me a girl? Did I do something wrong? I feel like a boy and I want to be a boy." Now, I have to tell you, the thought that Jordan could be a transgender child never entered my mind. In fact, I did not even know what it meant to be transgender at that time. I just presumed I had a very strong tomboy on my hands and I was totally okay with that. I did my best to reassure my daughter that girls were just as great as boys and that just because she was a girl it was okay to enjoy some of the things boys like to do. There was absolutely nothing wrong with the fact she liked trucks and karate while her sister liked dolls and dance. I told Jordan she was a very cool girl and she shouldn't worry about the fact she liked different things than her sister did. I told her that it was who she was and we loved her just the way she was.

I wasn't going to force her to take dance lessons or force her to wear a dress when I saw how visibly distraught those activities made her. Now, do not misunderstand me, I did introduce her to those things and not just by watching her older sister. As I shared earlier, I signed both my daughters up for dance, it just became a love for one and torture for the other. As a parent, I quickly realized that both our girls had strong wills, opinions, likes and dislikes and I felt it was my job to help guide them, not over power them. So, as long as their choices in clothes, toys, extra curricular activities and friends were not harming them in any way, Jim and I felt it best to allow their free will to flow. This seemed to keep harmony in the home and the family. We had a girly girl and a tomboy, both healthy and happy. Now let's be honest, isn't that really all we want as parents; healthy happy kids?

Birthdays were especially challenging for our tomboy. Each year we would set out to throw a fun birthday party for her whether it was bowling, karate, or just fun and games at home. However, what was difficult for my daughter Jordan was that her friends never seemed to fully understand her dislike for all things girly. She was always all smiles and very polite and outwardly appreciative of any gifts she received at her birthday parties, but in the end there were always a pile of gifts she would never play with or truly appreciate. I remember being so proud of how she would handle it. As she would open these gifts, that I knew were not resonating with her, she still remembered to thank her friends and put on a happy face.

I guess I should not have been surprised that each year it seemed like a battle to celebrate her birthday. I would ask her, "What would you like to do for your birthday this year?" The answer was always the same: "Nothing". Of course, we tried to communicate the fact that the birthday girl was a tomboy on the invitations, but that didn't always get through. Jordan's older sister Mariah was often the benefactor of all this mismatched gifting. That was because our tomboy would see it as an opportunity to barter for favours or even money, selling the girly girl gifts to her older sister. Then she would take that money to shop for what she really wanted, like remote control cars and army men. If my memory serves me well, I would have to say that her ninth birthday was the last year there was a real party. After that, we accepted her desire to celebrate only with family. This seemed rather sad to me year after year, but it was what Jordan wanted and we respected that.

CHAPTER 2

Teachers & Strangers

People often looked at Jordan's short hair and choice of clothing and just presumed she was a boy. There was an instance I remember well that occurred around the time Jordan was six years old. At the request of the girls, I signed Mariah and Jordan up for Rock Climbing camp for one week during the summer. I was happy they had found something they wanted to enjoy together. One day when I picked them up Mariah told me about how she had an argument with one of the teen counsellors who was trying to get Jordan to use the boys change room. I guess the counsellor assumed, due to Jordan's appearance, that she was a boy. Mariah said she was unable to convince them otherwise. I had noted Jordan as a girl when I enrolled her. So, I was surprised that so much drama was created and I certainly did not like that Mariah was stuck in the middle of it all.

The next morning when I dropped them off I made sure everyone was clear on the fact that Mariah was correct. Jordan did belong in the girls change room with her sister because she was in fact a girl. The staff felt embarrassed and did apologize for the mistake. I did understand as I knew Jordan wouldn't be defending her gender and likely would have preferred to be known as a boy. It was because of situations like these that I worried about what other, perhaps more worrisome situations Jordan could be put in. That time Mariah was there to speak up for Jordan, but her big sister can't always be there.

The following summer there was another incident when our family was at a public visitor's center. We were sitting having lunch when Jordan got up to go to the restroom. The restroom entrance was within eyesight of our table and very close by so we allowed Jordan to go in by herself. Jordan entered the ladies restroom and a man innocently followed her in. Once inside, the lack of urinals likely quickly alerted the man to the fact he was in the ladies washroom as he quickly came back out. He had likely just seen Jordan, assumed he was following a young boy into a male restroom. Jordan came out laughing, telling us how the man followed her into the ladies room because he assumed she was a boy. As humorous as this was at the moment, it was a little disconcerting to me. These situations, while they have been harmless so far, could have some unanticipated consequences in the future.

Each new school year was interesting. Our youngest, preferring ball caps, jeans and t-shirts was easily taken for a boy in public and that included school. Each year I would make a point of visiting the school on the first day and introduce my daughter by name saying "this is my daughter Jordan" and in the very next sentence the teacher would often use a male pronoun in referring back to my daughter. It didn't help that Jordan's name is non gender specific. One year I remember introducing Jordan to her grade 4 teacher "this is my daughter Jordan." The teacher said: "It's nice to meet you, Jordan. He can go ahead and hang his backpack over there." Wow, okay, let's try this again. "Jordan is my daughter, she is a huge tomboy who loves ball caps and jeans but Jordan is a girl." The teacher did apologize just like all the other teachers had when they made this same mistake. The school year would be just fine after that.

The teacher Jordan had in grade four turned out to be a wonderfully kind and encouraging teacher. She is someone our family became friends with after Jordan left elementary school and we still remain friends to this day. It was only years later this teacher shared a story with us about one day when she had asked Jordan's class to line up. She asked that the girls line up on the right and the boys on the left and remembered how Jordan just placed herself smack dab in the middle of the two lines, not committing to stand in either. I kind of wish I had heard that story from her back when Jordan was in that class, but like I said, it was only many years later this story was shared with us. It does offer some interesting insight though as to how Jordan was feeling back then.

I tried to talk Jordan into letting her hair grow out so there would be fewer situations where she was confused for a boy, but she was not at all interested in that idea. So, in the end, I forced Jordan to get her ears pierced as she was so unwilling to let her hair grow. I hoped that having her ears pierced would at least reduce some of the confusion when people looked at her. This is a decision I regret today. I never should have forced this on her. I was just so frustrated and worried about her safety that it felt like a good idea at the time. A couple weeks before Jordan's eighteenth birthday it was shared with Jim and me that Jordan very purposely pulled the backings off the earrings and threw them away in an effort to avoid wearing them. According to Jordan they were thrown in the park, hidden behind the tires on our vehicles (in the hopes we would run over them) and discarded on the walk to school. Now I know the real truth behind all those replacements I had to keep buying. I guess Jordan wasn't as careless as I thought back then, but instead just one creative and determined little kid.

Years later when transgender was on our radar, we were speaking with a doctor about it and one of the questions we were asked was "as a young child when Jordan was confused for being male did she ever correct?" The truth is she never did! It was only ever Jim, I or even Mariah that did the correcting; pointing out Jordan was a girl. Thinking back I can only remember the smile that would come over Jordan's face when someone would mistake her for a boy. It was like she was thinking either "ah, fooled another one" or "finally, someone gets me." Jim even recalls a time when he and Jordan were shopping for a mother's day gift for me. When Jordan pointed out the item she wished to buy to the sales clerk, the sales clerk replied: "Your mom is very lucky to have such a thoughtful son." Just smiling happily at this, Jordan never corrected the error.

There are times today when I wish I looked into the behaviour more, investigated more, spoke to our family doctor about it, but honestly, Jordan was happy. I really never knew anything about transgenderism so I guess in my mind there was nothing to look into. Now, I think there are tomboys and there are just boys. Family members and close friends have always tried to reassure me that we did a good job as parents and that Jordan was happy as a young child because we allowed for self expression and didn't force girly stereotypes on Jordan. Jim and I just assumed we had a hard core tomboy.

I look back now and I realize just how fortunate we were to be surrounded by extended family who loved both our children unconditionally for all their individuality and differences. No one tried to interfere and tell us how to raise our girls differently. I think this was because for them it was obvious they were equally loved, cherished and well cared for.

All in all, childhood seemed a happy place for both our children. I believe this was largely due to the fact that their father and I allowed them to be themselves.

CHAPTER 3

An Effort to Conform

"Being who you are is so much more important than fitting in will ever be."
~ Cheryl B. Evans

Jordan had good friends and a pleasant, easy going, personality, unless you tried to get her to wear a dress or do anything girly. Jordan had a talent for basketball and represented her school on the girls' basketball team during grades five, six and seven. I remember the first couple of games, the other parents wondered why there was a boy allowed on the team. Not realizing of course, there was no boy on the team. There was however, my tomboy daughter who seemed to have fooled them all. Midway through grade six is when things really became interesting. Puberty was starting and Jordan was noticing things were changing. This was a scary time for Jordan, realizing it was not going to be easy pretending to be a boy for much longer.

At some point Jordan started to think about making some changes and shocked us all with a single trip to the mall. Jordan came home from school and asked me if I would take her and her girlfriend to the mall. She was in grade six at the time. She told me she wanted her girlfriend to come along to help her pick out some new clothes. Going to the mall was not a regular thing for Jordan so that request seemed a little out of character. None the less, I granted her wish and took both girls shopping the following day. At the mall, it quickly became apparent to me that the true purpose of the trip was to 'girly' up my tomboy. I was surprised to see them picking out clothes for Jordan that she never would have been drawn to before. She came home with a couple girly t-shirts, a purple and black checked mini skirt, some new shoes with a small black bow on top and even a training bra. I have to admit I was surprised but a bit pleased at the same time. It was nice to see her dressing like a girl. She began to grow her hair longer and all the while I'm thinking to myself, she has finally decided to leave the tomboy behind and embrace being a girl. I was happy about that. She had outgrown the tomboy phase. After all, that's what it was a phase right?

No one was happier with the new Jordan than her older sister Mariah. Mariah had longed for the day when her sister would finally be the sister she had imagined way back when Jordan was born. Now, they could finally be on the same page, or so we all thought. The girls began to share clothes and Mariah showed Jordan how to put on makeup. They seemed closer than ever. We took a family vacation that winter during which we had some family photos taken in our formal attire. Both my girls looked gorgeous in their high heels and dresses. Back at home Jordan's teachers and friends all responded positively to her new girly look. The first time my father saw Jordan he was carrying a pie and almost dropped it on the floor, not because he didn't like the change, but it was just so unexpected. Even our extended family and friends welcomed the change.

The thing was, it didn't take long to see the biggest change in Jordan and it wasn't a positive one. It was like the life was being sucked out of her. She became withdrawn and antisocial, the complete opposite of the child we had always known. It seemed the only person not adjusting well to the new Jordan, was Jordan. You could see it even in photographs we had taken that winter when on vacation. It was like the lights in her eyes had been turned out. Looking back, I think the fact that we were all so happy Jordan wasn't a tomboy anymore, kept us from seeing the truth. We just weren't seeing how Jordan was doing. It wasn't for a lack of signs, they were there. It was for a lack of sight. Jordan was putting on a giant façade and we were too blind to see through it. At least we were at first.

Soon the signs became more prevalent. Jordan would hide out in her room for hours at a time, mope around the house, staring down at the floor and hardly engaging in conversation. She was a different child, a sad child. Other people began to notice how withdrawn she had become. As the year drew to a close, we had a very unhappy girl on our hands. Jordan's antisocial behaviour and depression grew stronger with each passing month. Jim and I tried to talk to her but she would just dismiss us and retreat to her room. Before Jordan changed her gender expression when friends come around to visit, which was often, she was happy to see them. Now, whenever someone came to the door for her she would say she was tired or didn't feel like socializing. We tried to shelter Mariah from much of what we saw and because she was now well into high school and busy with her own life we were able to do just that. However, that too, didn't last.

CHAPTER 4

A Cry For Help

Everyone's life matters and everyone deserves to be happy but not everyone is in a place where they think, or even believe, happiness is possible. We can't always see the scars people carry nor can we know how deep someone's scars go. Some suffer a pain so deep it may never surface but if it does, even if only for a moment, we need to listen. We need to act diligently for that person's very life may depend on it.

I'll never forget the call from the school that came telling us that a school psychologist had been called in to speak to Jordan. We were told the psychologist was on their way at that moment, and we should come right over. Once Jim and I arrived, we learned that Jordan had started cutting herself and was hiding it from us all. Luckily, she had confided in a friend and that friend told the principal. This same friend also told the principal that Jordan had also confided in her that she had already tried to kill herself. Apparently, Jordan had taken a bunch of Advil a month or so earlier, which resulted in a failed suicide attempt. This was the first we had heard about the suicide attempt, which we also learned from the principal. Jordan's friend had done the right thing, the brave thing, when she spoke up. We are so grateful she knew when to break a friend's trust. Jordan had chosen the right friend to confide in. That day was the day that changed everything! It was Jordan's cry for help and we were not going to ignore it.

When we got home Jordan finally opened up to her father and me about everything including the pills and the cutting. She said she had been unhappy for awhile now and just didn't think she could continue to live this way anymore. My immediate reply was, no problem, just go back to dressing how you were comfortable dressing before, you don't have to be a girly girl, but there was more. Jordan told us she had been researching on the internet and believed she knew what was the matter. She told us she believed she was transgender. She said she was a boy trapped in a girl's body and could not continue to live as a girl any longer. Our journey began that day; a journey that led us on a search for knowledge and answers.

Jordan told us that the only reason she was trying so hard to be a girl by growing out her hair and dressing differently, than she had in the past, was because she believed it is what 'we' wanted, what 'we' expected. Our positive reactions to the change certainly would have reinforced that thought. Today, it gives me some solace knowing she did try to live the way society expects, she truly tried to conform and she failed. As a parent, it is heart wrenching to see your children in pain. It is frightening to think of your child being in a place that is so dark that they feel the only way out is death.

I witnessed such a strong personality change in Jordan and it was difficult to watch. Jordan really was an incredibly happy-go-lucky kid, up until puberty started to rear its head that is. Puberty was a time when Jordan could no longer negate the fact she was a biological girl. Physical changes were beginning to happen and Jordan was not handling those changes well. I know now from the knowledge I've since gained that while puberty is challenging for most, it is pure hell for a transgender person.

My husband and I listened intently to our daughter Jordan as she poured her heart out to us in tears. We vowed to help her figure this out, whatever that meant. My first reaction was this is just a typical teenage girl going through puberty; her body chemistry is all over the map. Emotions are running high and low due to all the additional hormones rushing through her body and that in a few years we can revisit the idea of her being transgender if that's what this is. My advice to my daughter was to just take it slow; after all you're only thirteen years old. Step one; let's get professional advice, and someone she can talk to, heck, someone we can all talk to.

Meanwhile, I'm thinking of Mariah and how much she has loved having a true sister this year. This is going to rock her world. We decided it was best to hold off discussing the possibility of Jordan being transgender with Mariah or anyone else for that matter until we figured this out. There was no sense in telling the rest of the family until we were certain.

Jordan began meeting with the school board therapist right away, but she would just not open up. I'm not sure if it was the person or the fact that she was related to the school that Jordan was uncomfortable with but I knew she was never going to get the help she needed if she was not able to tell the person counselling her that she was having gender confusion issues.

So, we got a referral from our city's health department to a therapist who specializes in transgender issues and started scheduling appointments for Jordan on a regular basis. At the very first meeting, before the therapist would see Jordan, she wanted to speak to Jim and me alone. The very first question she asked us was: "What do you want to be achieved here?" My husband and I almost simultaneously said: "We just want a healthy happy child." The therapist's response was somewhat surprising to us. She said: "What a relief it is to hear you say that. There are so many parents who come in here and say just fix it." Really? This surprised me. Don't all parents want a healthy and happy child above all else? Over these last few years, I've come to realize that Jordan is one of the lucky ones, and I'm grateful to God for the privilege of allowing me to be Mom to this wonderful soul.

Once Jordan started with the new therapist we began to notice positive changes. Slowly but surely, Jordan seemed less depressed as the weeks went on. Part of it was likely the relief of having someone to talk to that was non judgemental and willing to listen. After each session, my husband and I would be called in and given an opportunity to ask questions or have our own concerns addressed (in general of course, as we respected the confidentiality of the sessions with Jordan). The three of us would work through our issues together with the therapist and each of us gaining insight into how the other was feeling. I felt the sessions were going very well and progress was being made.

Jordan's mood continued to improve and the darkness continued to lighten. It wasn't long before the therapist told us that she believed Jordan was, in fact, transgender. It was months later after continuing to see Jordan that the therapist told Jim and me that after years and years of working with transgender patients, Jordan was the clearest cut case she had ever seen. Jordan liked his therapist and felt very comfortable opening up to her. At this time, even though the therapist would continue to counsel Jordan, we felt it was our responsibility to seek out the advice of other medical professionals. We quickly learned finding the right doctor isn't always an easy task.

PART TWO

The Quest for Truth and Knowledge

CHAPTER 5

Health, Doctors and Hormones

When it comes to working with medical professionals it is very important to find those who have experience working with transgender people. It is my understanding that doctors get less than a few hours on the subject of transgenderism during their entire four years of medical school. During the clinical studies that follow (which can be another two to four years) their transgender education depends solely on whether or not they are working in an environment where they are exposed to transgender patients and their care. Many family doctors have never treated a transgender person, even after years of practice, so finding a doctor with that experience may require some research. It did for us.

It is important that the doctor you are consulting with will be able to distinguish a transgender patient from a patient who may actually not be transgender at all. One of the more common clues found in a transgender person is their gender identity can be traced back to early childhood. Even when a transgender person waits till much later in life to transition they can usually trace back their feelings to when they were much younger. Without a knowledgeable doctor to consult with, it is possible a person can confuse their feelings of being transgender with something else and vice versa. Though at this point, based on Jordan's therapy sessions, it was more a medical confirmation we were looking for. It took me a couple of weeks to find a family doctor in our area that had experience treating transgender people. When I first reached out to his office, I was told he wasn't accepting new patients. After being turned away by phone, I wrote a letter explaining the challenging time I was having finding a doctor that had experience with transgender patients and that his name was given to me by a colleague of his. I explained that my child is struggling with gender identity issues and it was important that we find a family doctor that had experience in this area. The initial response was still no. I was told his practice was simply too full. It took some haggling and some determined phone calls but I finally broke through. In the end, the doctor agreed to make an exception and opened his practice to Jordan. Determination paid off.

Once Jordan had settled in with this new family doctor he too concurred with the therapist's opinion that Jordan was transgender. He was able to refer us to an endocrinologist (specialist in hormones and genes) who, in the end, offered the same medical conclusion; a transgender diagnosis. The medical term is actually gender dysphoria.

Jordan was in what I can only describe as a state of relief

when the endocrinologist concurred with the transgender diagnosis. The endocrinologist, even with his experience having over four hundred transgender patients in his practice wanted to do his own due diligence. He wanted Jordan to see a psychiatrist for one more evaluation just to ensure there was nothing the other medical professionals, himself included, had overlooked.

The psychiatrist concurred with the previous transgender diagnosis given by the other medical professionals Jordan had seen. After seeing multiple doctors in multiple cities and feeling like all our 'T's were crossed and our 'I's dotted, Jim and I began to see the light and the end of what had been a very dark road for our child. It felt as if this crazy ride was almost over, but the truth was, our journey was only just beginning.

Once a person starts on the path to transition there are many permanent changes that simply cannot be reversed, so you need to be certain before proceeding. A good doctor will likely refer their patient for a second opinion with a specialist before proceeding with any course of action. Just as Jordan's new family doctor did.

Once Jordan's own feelings about being transgender were confirmed by his doctors, we needed a plan. At this point, Jordan had been in therapy for more than seven months and was now looking forward to the process of transitioning getting under way.

It was the last week of November and the Endocrinologist

had prescribed two medications for Jordan. The first was called Suprefact Nasal. This was a nasal spray to be sprayed into each nostril two times a day (morning and night). This was going to stop Jordan's female hormones from allowing puberty as a female to continue. Jordan's menstrual periods would stop (which they did after six weeks on the spray) and Jordan's breasts would stop developing. The Suprefact Nasal would need to be taken for as long as Jordan continues to have a uterus and ovaries. The second drug was Delatestryl (200 MG/ML) commonly known as testosterone, taken via injection once every two weeks. This would need to be taken for the rest of Jordan's life. Testosterone is the male hormone that causes the voice to drop, a pronounced Adam's apple to appear, muscular structure to change, and hair to grow on the face, chest and other areas typical for males.

Of course, there were questions and we asked many, believe me! What were the side effects of being on Suprefact Nasal for a prolonged period of time? What about organ damage? How would it affect his liver, for example? Would Jordan experience mood swings or become aggressive because of the testosterone? How soon would Jordan's voice start to change? This is just a small sampling of the questions we asked and researched. We wanted to ensure we were going in with our eyes wide open, and had knowledge of all the facts.

Before starting Jordan on any medications, his family doctor did a complete physical, including a full blood panel which included checking all hormone levels and Jordan's liver. We wanted to ensure we had a baseline reference point from which to monitor Jordan's health moving forward. It wasn't until after all the test results came back that we had the prescriptions filled and Jordan started on his hormone replacement therapy (HRT). We needed to wait until the results were reviewed by both the family doctor and the Endocrinologist. The results showed that everything was normal and within a healthy range.

Jordan was in good physical health. We had already started to see positive changes in his emotional health as a result of both his continued therapy sessions and the confirmation of a transgender diagnosis. As parents, Jim and I still had concerns. After all, Jordan was only thirteen. I had countless heart to heart talks with Jordan, trying to explain the concerns we had which, for the most part, related to Jordan's age. We were not the ones living in Jordan's body, but we were the ones responsible for his well being. I could not help but think how smart I thought I was when I was thirteen or fourteen years of age, only to realize in my twenties how little I really knew back then. The teenage years were tough to live through, but as a parent, for me anyway; the teen years have been far more challenging to parent through. It's that great perspective thing. You just do not have it from where you are right now. It is only when you move beyond where you are in years you can look back and see what you only wish you could have seen at the time. There was really nothing more I could say at this point. Jordan's mind was made up and there was no dissuading him.

If you are going to transition, is there ever really a good time to start? We explored this question a lot with Jordan's regular therapist. We discovered there really is no perfect time, but some times are definitely going to be easier than others. I was thinking of Jordan's age and if I'm completely honest, perhaps my own desire to slow things down. This was all just so much to take in. We discussed waiting until Jordan was in college. The therapist pointed out that while I might feel better with that because Jordan would be older; the fact is college is a challenging time. During college, there are already expected pressures from heavy study loads, relationships, and jobs. Adding the pressure of transitioning to the mix, at that time, could be far more overwhelming than it would be earlier. For Jordan, the idea of waiting was terrible.

He wanted to start now so that by the time he turned sixteen and was ready to apply for his first job (outside of babysitting), or his driver's licence, he would be able to do those things like any other teenager. He could avoid the entire stigma that could come with having to explain everything. I could definitely empathize with that. It was also explained that if top surgery was something we were going to consider down the road that a surgeon would not do the surgery unless the patient had been on the transgender drugs for a year or more. Any delay in not starting the medication would also result in Jordan continuing to go through puberty as a female. This would make female characteristics more predominant and make transitioning later more complicated.

At this stage, Jordan's breasts had only begun to form so binding the chest was not difficult. (At the end of this book I will provide a list of references for you, including a place where transgender binders can be purchased.) A female to male chest binder looks just like a tank top with very tight binding fabric that literally flattens out the chest. When Jordan wore a binder under his t-shirts he presented with a flat male looking chest.

Jordan was so certain about whom he was, and very strong willed about this. He was a boy and he knew it. For him, it was as obvious as the sky being blue. When I expressed our concerns about his age and allowing him to make this decision at such a young age, he always had an answer. I worried that later, from a different perspective, he might regret it. After all, he was only thirteen. He just kept assuring me that that wouldn't happen. Jordan would tell me that while this seemed all new in the last year or so to his dad and me, for him it has been what he has felt and known on the inside since his earliest memories.

The reason I think Jordan was such a happy kid was that in the early years before hormones and puberty it was easy for him just to be himself. The fact that he did try to conform, in the previous year, did help show us all that being female was just not going to be possible for Jordan. Jordan even said to me: "You know Mom, it's not like I want this. I know it's not going to be easy but for me what you need to understand is that the alternative is impossible." The alternative was, of course, to live life as a girl.

I really did know in my heart of hearts that for Jordan it was a live life as his authentic self or not live at all scenario. I remember not too long into Jordan's regular therapy appointments, his therapist asked him just how certain he was that he was male and wanted to make this transition on a percentage scale of 1-100%. Jordan answered 95%. When asked what the 5% was that was keeping him from being certain, he replied that this was something that would be difficult for his family. He said the 5% holding him back was that he didn't want to hurt his family. She asked Jordan to answer the question again, but this time disregard the family part. He replied 100%. He was 100% sure he was male and wanted to transition.

I think we all need to realize that the way we react to someone telling us they are transgender is critically impactful, especially to children. It is difficult for a cisgender person like myself to conceptualize being trapped in a different body and comprehend how that might feel. I imagine if I woke up one morning and looked down and my breasts were gone and I saw a penis I would be like "what the hell," get me out of here. That would not line up at all with how I feel on the inside. Human beings are so interconnected and our relationships are very complex. It is easy for us to influence others; even put incredible pressure on others, with our expectations without necessarily realizing how damaging that is to someone we love.

To think my child would consider taking his own life or live his life in complete torment just to protect my feelings or live up to social expectations is heart breaking. I would never want someone I love to live a life they hated or one that causes them this level of distress for the sake of keeping harmony with another. Yet, so many parents find themselves struggling with this. They do not want a transgender child; maybe they don't believe it is a real thing, maybe they believe it's not what God intended. Maybe they believe it will be socially awkward. It can be a struggle; there is no question about that. What I want to challenge parents to look at is not their struggle but their child's struggle.

They didn't ask for this, they did not want to have a life path that would be so challenging. They just are who they are. If you have found yourself in this position I encourage you to find an outlet, learn all you can and talk to your child. It's okay to be hurt, sad, worried and, yes, even scared; I felt all of those things. My child is alive, he is healthy and I want him to have a great life, even if it was not the one I had envisioned for him.

CHAPTER 6

A New Reality

At this point, Jim and I had conceded to the fact that this was really happening. There was no longer a question as to whether or not Jordan was transgender. It was now time to be there for Jordan. Jim and I wanted to do what we could as parents to make Jordan's transition as smooth as possible. There was so much to consider. I could not help but wonder how the rest of the family would take the news? How about Jordan's school? Would the principal, the teachers, and students be accepting? There was also a young boy that Jordan babysat on a regular basis, whose parents would need to be told. Before we got to all of them, there was someone far more important to discuss all this with. First, it was time to tell *his* sister.

This was extremely difficult for me as a mother. I knew at this point that I had to support Jordan. It truly was a matter of life or death. However, in helping Jordan, I knew I was going to be stirring things up for Mariah. In order to help one child, I knew I would be hurting another. This felt terrible, and was much more difficult than I had imagined it would be. I just kept reminding myself that it was all about happy healthy children, that is what I wanted. The only thing was that at the time, I had no idea just how long this road would be or how difficult it would be emotionally for our family. Believing that, one day, both our children would be happy again is what kept me moving forward. Telling Mariah about our intention to help Jordan transition was the next step.

I took my beautiful daughter Mariah out to dinner and although she was not completely out of the loop as to the happenings around our family, she was protected from much of the goings on. Mariah was now in her last year of high school and I could not have been more proud of her and the incredible young woman she was becoming. I knew this was going to be hard for her to take but I told her as gently as I could that we were now confident that Jordan was in fact transgender and that soon we would be beginning the process of helping him transition from female to male.

At this point, out of respect for Jordan, Jim and I had already begun trying to use male pronouns, even though we would sometimes slip up. It is not easy when you have been addressing someone as female for over thirteen years to suddenly switch and address them as male. It took some time to adjust. Now, it was time to ask Mariah if she felt she could endeavour to do the same. I felt like I was breaking her heart. She cried and I felt helpless knowing only time would likely heal her wounds. Mariah said that she had waited years for her sister to finally show up and she was enjoying having a real sister for the first time. Mariah said: "It's like she just got here and now you are taking her away."

That's really what it was like for all of us, Jordan excluded of course. Jim and I had to mourn the loss of a daughter and learn to welcome a son. Mariah had to mourn the loss of a sister and learn to welcome a brother. Of course Jordan was still the same person, but yet in some way wasn't. It was an adjustment for all of us. Although the transition didn't seem to affect Jim quite the same as the way it did Mariah and me. Jim was always so much more composed about everything. Mariah and me in comparison were much more emotional.

One thing I can definitely say for certain is that when the decision was made to help Jordan become the male he had always known himself to be, the light came back into his eyes. The darkness seemed to lift and Jordan's true personality, the one that shone so brightly when he was younger, began to return. Jordan stopped hiding out in his room and rejoined the conversation. He held his head high again and appeared hopeful for his future.

Mariah did step up to the plate and was the wonderful big sister she'd always been, but not before she had her doubts. Mariah was always protective of Jordan and I think that came into play when we first told her this was a reality. As I'd mentioned earlier we did shelter her from things so she was never fully aware of all the doctors' and specialists' appointments we were keeping. Initially, she questioned our parenting and whether or not we had looked at all the possibilities before accepting a transgender diagnosis. I tried very hard to reassure her we had. Her genuine concern for her sibling made me love her even more.

Transgenderism is a hard thing for many to understand and is often confused with sexual preference or orientation rather than pure gender identity. Knowing someone's gender does not speak to their sexual orientation. At the end of this book, I go into some of the terminology that may offer further insight. We did get some interesting responses when we began discussing Jordan's situation with others because, just like me in the beginning, not everyone is well versed on the topic.

In a search for answers Mariah reached out to a couple that she barely knew but that were strong Christians and she felt they might be able to offer her some answers. The couple she reached out to had only met Jordan once, very briefly, and really knew nothing about our family or the childhood Jordan had had. Nevertheless, they did have something to say when asked if they believed Jordan could be transgender. They told Mariah that what she was describing was 'not of God'. Those three words 'not of God' hurt our family more than I care to admit. It took months, even years; to undue the damage those three words did to our family. Jordan and Mariah went from being very close to almost avoiding each other. A home often filled with laughter was void of it. It was a very difficult time, a heart wrenching time and I cried myself to sleep many nights.

I was mad and upset for a long time at how two people who were only loosely acquainted with my family could have even offered such a strong opinion to my daughter. I could feel myself becoming very defensive just like a momma bear looking out for her cubs. There were so many times I bit my tongue and kept silent as I watched others pour their influence over my daughter. I could not help but think they were filling her head with doubt, shame and judgement. It was likely not as bad as my active imagination was making it out to be, but it still made me feel helpless and angry.

Mariah took many trips to visit friends, many with strong religious faiths. This is what worried me most, and it felt like I was losing her. I felt Mariah pulling away but all I could do was pray that the day would come when she could accept Jordan as a brother. It seemed she was happiest when she wasn't at home. There was no doubt it was a very difficult time for Mariah. Deep down I knew that what I saw as running away was just her way of dealing with things. Being away from home was likely what she needed most and I had to trust her. I needed to believe she would not let others come between us, and I did that, but it wasn't easy. As her mom, I was feeling insecure. I was jealous of the many seemingly adoptive moms she appeared to be gravitating to. They were the ones she went to. The ones she shared her innermost thoughts with, not me. This made me sad. I missed her so much during that time.

I could not help but think I had disappointed her, that I wasn't enough. Getting your ego bruised is never a fun experience but it is humbling. I longed for the day when she and I could connect on a deeper level. Mothers and daughters seem to go through stages in life. That has been my own experience with my mother and history seems to be repeating itself with Mariah and me. Thinking back, I wasn't unlike her when I was in my late teens. I also shared my own secrets with anyone but my own mom. Then, later in my twenties, I somehow found my way back and my mom became one of my closest friends. After becoming a mother myself, it somehow deepened the relationship between my mother and I even more. I suspect that is how it is for a lot of mothers and daughters.

Not everyone was blindly spewing advice at Mariah. There were others that she reached out to, close family friends, that at least had a better understanding of our family and also knew Jordan when he was younger. These caring individuals did what I hope anyone in their situation would do; they referred Mariah back to her parents. They lovingly explained that no one would have Jordan's best interest at heart more than her father and I would and that Mariah should trust us and talk to us about her concerns. You see it didn't matter what these individuals personally thought about the situation or about transgender people as a whole. What mattered was that they empathized and cared for my daughter without introducing her to, or bringing to her, any more confusion or pain. They didn't stir the pot and for that, I am very thankful.

Mariah needed love and support not doubt and judgement. She is a very private person in many ways. She doesn't like being centered out and she hates confrontation. The changes in our family were taking their toll on her. I asked Mariah one day how she was feeling about everything and she told me that while she understood she didn't agree with what her father and I were doing, referring to us helping Jordan to transition. Hearing her say those words wounded me. I was frozen and didn't know how to respond. To this day, I've never asked her that question again. I am afraid it would break my heart if she still felt that same way.

It is natural to want to know why someone is transgender, to ask, why is this happening? Trying to find a cause or someone to blame is pointless and can only cause more pain. There is some suggestive science out there but nothing written is irrefutable about why someone is transgender. Looking for the answer to why could literally drive a person crazy. If you are struggling, the sooner you can move past the why, and onto acceptance, the better. It is only after acceptance that you, your child and your family can move forward. In acceptance, everyone can begin to find peace. I believe Buddha summed it up best when he said,

"Serenity comes when you trade expectations for acceptance".

~ Buddha

It was the end of November and Jordan's grade eighth year. It was two years from the time Jordan had changed his outward appearance from that of a tomboy to typical teenage girl. I have very few pictures of Jordan during these two years primarily because of Jordan's resistance to having his photo taken during this time. A resistance to having pictures taken didn't exist in the earlier part of Jordan's childhood. Then again, Jordan's outward appearance in childhood reflected what was being felt inward. If you were to see Jordan today, you would see someone who loves having their photo taken. Jordan today is clearly a person very comfortable with how he looks and feels in his own skin, such a blessing to witness.

CHAPTER 7

What Does God Think?

Even though in my heart I knew that Jordan was in fact a transgender male, I could not help but wonder; what does God think?

I consider myself a spiritual person and I do believe in God. If ever there was a time in my life where I needed some divine reassurance, it was then. At the time I had been working with a life coach, a strong woman of God, who I felt compelled to turn to for advice. Her advice was to refer me to a trusted family friend and counsellor that she herself had used to work through some issues in her own life. The funny thing is I had heard this coach say, on numerous occasions, "Look to Me, Not to Man" as advice to always turn to God first for answers. On this day however she didn't turn me to God she turned me to man. Actually, woman would be more accurate as it was a female counsellor she recommended I contact. I went ahead and called the counsellor my coach had referred me to and almost immediately got a weird feeling that this was a mistake. Intuition is a crazy thing and I am learning to trust mine more and more as the years go on.

The conversation went on for over an hour with me doing

very little talking. I explained that we believed our daughter Jordan was actually a transgender male and we were about to embark on the journey of helping him transition to his true self. The initial response was that she was glad I had called and that she could definitely help me and help Jordan to love her female self. She proceeded to refer me to scripture after scripture in the Bible. It is amazing that I was able to write them all down because I was crying so hard. I did manage to share the story of Mariah confiding in a couple who told her that being transgender was 'not of God'. She said I should not worry, that we could "fix" Jordan. The thing was the decision to "fix" Jordan was almost an automatic response. It was not a conclusion that was arrived at after a long look into Jordan, Jordan's history or even Jordan's current state of mind. Heck, this person had never even laid eyes on Jordan and I certainly wasn't being given an opportunity to provide much information during the call. I could hardly get a word in the entire time. It was obvious to me that the circumstances didn't matter. It was a case of her mind already being made up that there was no such thing as a transgender person and this child just needed fixed. She wanted to schedule another call at the end, but I declined saying I'd have to get back to her on that. Of course, I never did.

After the call ended I just sat alone in my bedroom and wept like a baby. Then I prayed. I prayed in the morning and I prayed in the evening. I have never prayed so hard. "Please God, help me understand, help us make the right decisions for Jordan, help us do the right thing." When I prayed, I heard the same message again and again "Help Your Son," "Help Your Son." Of course, God would surely know Jordan better than anyone else and certainly better than some counsellor who barely asked me anything about Jordan's childhood, our family or our life. I continued to pray and God continued to deliver me only one message "Help Your Son." Okay! I hear you.

The Bible is an interesting book that is used by so many to prove a point this way or that way. I did something few people actually do. I set out to read it for myself, word for word, paragraph by paragraph, page by page, chapter by chapter. Perhaps, saying book by book would be more accurate than chapter by chapter when discussing the Bible. Regardless, I expect you get my point which is that I approached it the same way I approach any other book. My reading included both the Old and New Testaments. It took me seven months to complete it. Even though I felt a sense of accomplishment when I was finished, I recognized that having read the Bible in no way made me an expert on it. I am not prepared to try to formally debunking religious theory or confirm it. However, I did make some interesting observations while reading it. In my opinion, there appears to be many inconsistencies within the Bible. Biblical text is difficult for a layman like me to decipher. To thoroughly understand it, you have to not just read the words in the sentences but look at the context of those sentences. You need to be aware of the smallest nuances and even give consideration to the person speaking. You must determine if the person speaking is testifying to their own account of events or are they quoting someone else. My point is that most people, if they study it long enough, can interpret any passage or combination of passages in such a way that it either supports their case or refutes someone else's.

For anyone who struggles with the Bible and believes that being transgender is against God, I found something that may be of interest. What I found was some interesting biblical teachings on eunuchs and eunuch prophecies. It is an in-depth Bible study, including flow charts, prepared by Brian Bowen Ministries and it can be found at www.eunuchflow.blogspot.ca. The main idea presented is that Jesus wants the churches to be all inclusive by inviting everyone in. The study suggests that until all people including LGBT people are treated the same as everyone else by the church, Jesus will not return.

The word of God says love thy neighbour, it doesn't say love thy neighbour except for the ones you do not like. There are non-gender conforming people in the Bible and God doesn't strike any of them dead, nor does Jesus turn away from them. It also says in the Bible that God looks at one's heart, not at one's outward appearance. I am not sure if you see gender when you think of God, but I don't. For me, when it says we were created in God's image, it's about having a heart and spirit like God. It is not about one's outer image or specific gender.

There are things in the Bible I disagree with. Conditions or practices that may have made sense back in biblical times, but today would be met with widespread disapproval. For example, men having multiple wives and fathering children from their multiple wives. How about girls marrying and giving birth when they themselves are still small children? That's all acceptable in the Bible. Here's a thought; if God didn't mean for girls to have babies at twelve and thirteen years of age, why did he make it so they could? In Biblical times, I believe it was necessary to populate for survival. To put it simply, there is strength in numbers. This was needed at the time to grow and defend one's territory. Under these circumstances, it made sense for one man to father multiple children with multiple wives. The reality is we do not live in biblical times.

Today, we enjoy benefits like modern medicine. Heart bypass surgery and pacemakers are two examples of how we can alter the outcome of one's life that were not available in biblical times. Does that mean just because modern medicine wasn't available back then that we shouldn't use it today? Some religions dictate exactly that. To live a modern day life on the literal teachings of the Bible, to me, seems ludicrous. I choose to live a life based on love and compassion towards my fellow human beings. If someone believes I'm doing a disservice to God in some way by doing that, well that's their issue, not mine. Having said that,

I also think it is worthy to note that I do have respect for others that have a different opinion and choose to follow a different path. I absolutely respect a person's right to have their own opinions, no matter how much I may disagree with those opinions. I believe that respecting another's rights to interpret the Bible and draw their own conclusion about what God wants for them is important. Provided of course, their own interpretations are not used as punishment against others. Using the Bible as a tool to manipulate, judge or condemn others seems to be little about love and more about hate to me. I do not believe God intended that to be the message.

I hope that this conveys to you that I am not out to challenge your religion or to have you turn away from that which you believe. I understand that religion plays a very important role and for some it can be at the very root of their soul. While not all religious people feel conflict, I bring it up because it saddens me deeply when I see the torment some families go through when they struggle with transgenderism and religion.

Why is it so easy to accept that people can be born with something extra, missing or mismatched like a limb but can't have something extra, missing or mismatched with their brain? Obviously, we can't 'see' the brain but we can clearly see where a limb is, or isn't meant to be. Seriously, though, just because we can't see something doesn't mean we should just assume it is as we expect it to be. Is it really impossible to believe that there could be something in the brain that doesn't align with the person's exterior?

I feel thankful that my beliefs allow me to accept that transgender people are not against God but I understand that not everyone shares my beliefs. What helps me to see transgender people as sharing an equal place among God's children is that I believe they were born that way. I also believe that love is the most important emotion of all. I have read many near death experience stories and there seems to be a common thread among them and that thread is love.

Religion, while it has its purpose and offers great comfort to many, it also has its weaknesses. I see rigidness in many religions that can block love and leave the door open for shame, fear and even hate. In addition to my belief in God, I also believe that we are all spiritual beings having a human experience. When I think of what a spiritual being is I do not see gender. Gender to me only comes into play in our human experience and because I believe this, accepting people of all genders, even genders that differ from their assigned gender at birth, is easy. I guess I'm fortunate to believe what I do as it certainly makes it easier for me to be there for my child without fear of God or fear of judgement of others.

If someone's beliefs make acceptance difficult for them, I hope they can find peace and love before permanent damage is done to their relationships. Perhaps seeking the guidance from their own spiritual counsellor may help. Accepting something and agreeing with it is not the same thing. Through love and compassion there is a way to accept things, even things we do not fully understand. A way to hopefully protect the relationship you have with any transgender person(s) in your life. I hope that would be your end goal, to find a way to protect your relationship and be able to continue to love that person regardless of your beliefs. God acknowledges each person has free will so, in order to live peacefully; we need to find a way to accept others as they are.

It may help to remember that no one lives their life according to the Bible. They can only live their life according to their 'interpretation' of the Bible. There's a big difference. We should embrace the fact that we are individual thinkers. We should question, study and learn for ourselves rather than blindly follow the interpretation of another. We all have different paths to follow, different purposes to fulfill and we cannot successfully do that if we do not exercise our own abilities to hear God's word for ourselves. Listen to the word for yourself, filter out the noise of others and draw on your own strength to interpret it for yourself.

I believe God loves ALL his children and by ALL I mean exactly that. My belief allows me to follow his direction "Help Your Son" without question. I turned to God and not to man, I got guidance and I chose to follow it. I no longer search for approval from others. My conscience is clear.

Some of my Christian friends who are unaware of my son's

history openly share their anti-LGBT thoughts with me. It is difficult for me trying to express my own thoughts and positions on the issues without being so passionate as to arouse suspicion about where my motivation is coming from. That may sound like I don't care about other members of the LGBT community, only my son. That's not true. However, when you are so close to a situation, there is a motivation that emanates from that, driving you to speak out; at least that's how it is for me personally.

Many of my friends have children and grandchildren of their own. I wonder if their own children or grandchildren were transgender, how they would handle it. Would they take them for therapy to "fix" them? Would they inquire about shock treatments and other invasive therapies that once were accepted but now discarded? How far down the path would they go before they reached acceptance? If it were their children or grandchildren that didn't fit into our binary definitions of male and female, would they put love first and rally together? These are good people, honest, caring people I am talking about. I want to believe their anti-LGBT, specifically anti-transgender positions would quickly crumble if they were talking about someone they love, but I honestly don't know if it would.

Jim and I believe in the church of family. Given the choice of loving and supporting a family member or adhering to the teachings of a church or religion, it is no contest. The family member and their well being will always be our priority. Sometimes the best way we can serve God is by honouring and taking care of that which has already been given to us. This, in my case, is my children. Today Jordan is healthy and strong. We love and accept him for exactly who he is, our son.

If you are a parent of a transgender child, especially if you are struggling with that reality, know that you are not alone. Whether you believe in God or not, believe in yourself. Believe that there is no one that knows your child the way you do. Believe that you are well equipped to love your child. At the root of it all, there must be love. You loved your child when they were born and you have loved them up to this point. Please continue to love them now and after they transition. Ignore the criticisms of others, they will criticize you regardless. We should be grateful our children are alive to love. We should be thankful we can continue to share our lives with them regardless of whether they are male or female. It is a heart wrenching time, for some more so than for others, but if you make it about love not gender, you will get through this journey; that, I can promise you.

CHAPTER 8

Worthy of Support

It is not necessary to support someone's position in order to support them, though it's wonderful if you do. Jordan's therapist thought it would be helpful for me to have another mom to talk to, someone who was going through the same things I was going through. I agreed and she connected me with another mom, (her name was Sandra). Sandra's son was about two years ahead of Jordan on this whole journey. It was a relief to have someone else to talk to that had already been through this or at least was further along than we were. Sandra was a huge comfort to me and very easy to talk to. She openly shared with me the struggles they had had. Sandra offered me advice about talking to Jordan about different things, including some uncomfortable things like binding and packing. I was still learning and glad for any help I could get.

I talked to Jordan about the possibility of meeting Sandra and her son Dillon (born Sarah) in person. I thought it would be good for Jordan to have another person who was going through the same things as he was to talk to. Jordan agreed so Sandra and I planned for the four of us to get together a few weeks later.

A few days before Jordan and I were to meet Sandra and Dillon I called to confirm but got Sandra's answering machine. I left a message saying how much Jordan and I were looking forward to meeting them both. We had planned to meet up at a restaurant but just hadn't finalized which one.

It was two days later when I got a call back, which was the day before we were to meet them. When Sandra called me back I could barely make out anything she was saying. After a minute or so I realized she was crying and sniffling into the phone making her words muttered and hard to understand. Eventually, she was able to compose herself enough to deliver to me unthinkable news. She was not going to be meeting with us the following day, for that day was now set aside for Dillon's funeral. Dillon had taken his own life just a few days before. Apparently, Dillon had been having a difficult time and was admitted to hospital. Sandra just kept saying they were supposed to be keeping an eye on him. She told me she had taken him to the hospital so he would be safe and get the help he needed. "They didn't look after him; they didn't keep him safe" she sobbed. Dillon had hanged himself in the shower and died at the tender age of sixteen. I was stunned, heartbroken, and honestly terrified. Could something like this happen to Jordan?

After I hung up the phone with Sandra, I called Jim to share the devastating news with him. He was immediately overcome with emotion. A magnitude of grief swept over him that seemed so disproportionate with what I had expected, given he had never spoken to either Sandra or her son Dillon.

I had shed many tears up to this point, but Jim had been a rock. He had been very logical and composed throughout this whole journey, at least before that day he was. Dillon's death brought all his emotions rushing to the surface. He sobbed uncontrollably and later told me he had felt as if he had a taste of what it would be like to actually lose a child. Jim's deep sadness stayed with him throughout that afternoon and it was the first time Jordan had ever seen his dad cry.

Jim shared with me how the news of Dillon's death had really hit home for him and that it really made him realize just how serious this situation with Jordan was. He worried that one misstep on our part could have the same devastating outcome. We could not let that happen!

I brought my concerns to Jordan's therapist but she told me that the situation with Dillon was nothing like it was for Jordan. She couldn't go into details of course, but did say their environments were not the same and unfortunately Dillon had had issues to face that Jordan did not.

I knew from my own conversations with Dillon's mom, Sandra, that his parents were separated and that his dad was not fully supportive of Dillon's transition from female to male. His schoolmates weren't always kind and these two things alone weighed heavily upon Dillon. Love and acceptance are two things we all need, and when someone is denied acceptance, especially a child from a parent, it can cause so much pain. We must love our children, we must accept them for who they are; to do anything less is unimaginable to me.

I am sad that Jordan and I never got to meet Dillon but I will always be grateful to him and his mother Sandra for being there for me in those early weeks and months. I tried reaching out to Sandra after Dillon's death but I think it was just too painful for her to maintain a friendship with me when one of the people that brought us together was no longer with us.

Fortunately for Jordan, he has the love and support of his parents as well as a good school and good friends who also support him. On this journey, I have learned that many transgender children are without the support and love they need. There are so many transgender youth on the streets or in foster care because their families turned them away. I learned of one teen in our own community whose parents threw them out into foster care when they presented as transgender. Just stop and think about that for a second. Family is the most basic and most important social unit we have and sadly for some kids that is being taken away and lost. The torment of realizing that your own family can't love you or care for you and can not tolerate you in their home is a brutal reality for far too many. What are these kids to think? If their own families have turned them away, how can they believe anyone out in the world will feel any differently?

I cannot think of a single thing that my kids could do that would prompt me to throw them out like that. Perhaps the families that turn their children away believe throwing a child out is a tough love approach to scaring the child straight, so to speak. Perhaps they turn them away for religious reasons or fear of public humiliation. Whatever the reason, the statistics today are scary. Suicide attempts among transgender youth is forty one percent versus only four percent among non-transgender youth. That's alarming. This percentage is even higher, over fifty percent, in transgender youth that do not have their families' support. Yes, we are making progress. The world is much more accepting than it was twenty years ago, but for those youth still treated as outcasts, it is of little comfort. No one said parenting was easy but turning away from a child because they have come out as transgender says far more about the parent than it does about the child. More loving, more accepting and less judging is what we so desperately need in this world today.

There was an afternoon, early on in Jordan's transition, when he was visibly upset and he just stormed out of the house without telling me he was leaving or where he was headed. The only reason I was even aware he had left was because I heard the back patio door shut. Initially, I just assumed he was out on the back deck. A short time later, I went to check on him and found he wasn't there. I called out for him but I got no answer. After checking the house and both the front and back yards, I realized he was gone.

I was worried about him so I tried calling his cell phone. I was hoping to calm him down and convince him to return home so we could talk it through, but he didn't answer. After about an hour, panic began to set in. Where the heck was he? What was he doing? Knowing he had tried to kill himself once before, my mind immediately went there. Was he so upset he might try to harm himself again? Feeling distraught, I paced the floor, calling his cell phone every couple of minutes but my calls kept going straight to his voicemail. I left messages begging him to call me back, but he didn't. Hearing the sheer panic in my voice, Jim went out to look for him.

I felt ill to my stomach. My pulse was racing, my heart was pounding and tears were streaming down my cheeks when Jim finally called to say he had found him and they were on their way home. Jordan had gone for a long walk and was sitting on a curb at the side of the road when his dad pulled up.

I was still blubbering like an idiot when Jordan walked through the front door. I threw my arms around him, squeezed him tight and told him I loved him. Then, I told him that he scared the crap out of me! I was so grateful he was home safe. He said he just needed some fresh air, some space to think and that he wanted to be alone. I don't think he realized that by just leaving without saying a word it would send me reeling into panic mode. As it turned out, he was okay. I still made him promise he would never just take off like that again without telling me where he was going or when he expected to be back.

If a person is questioning or confused about their gender identity it is important they have someone to talk to, preferably a trained professional therapist. It is equally important that their significant other, parents or family members do also. I know some people are very uncomfortable sharing their thoughts, feelings and struggles with a complete stranger, but it really can be helpful. Too often it is the ones that feel most alone that are at risk. If you think you know someone who is suffering, ensuring they have a sympathetic ear is a great way to help. In our situation, Jordan had a good therapist and I was fortunate to have close family and friends I could talk to. I tried to encourage Mariah to come to the therapist with us but she didn't want to. At the time she was almost eighteen and I didn't feel it was appropriate for me to force her to go.

Around that same time, I had discovered a friend I was close with back in high school had also had a transgender child. We had stayed in touch off and on over the years and were able to confide in each other. It helped immensely. We were both discovering and learning. Since neither of us was an expert, it was just comforting to have the ear of someone that would listen without judgement.

CHAPTER 9

It's A New Dawn

"With the new day comes new strength and new thoughts."
~ Eleanor Roosevelt

The time had come to figure out just exactly how all this would play out in Jordan's day to day life. There was a lot to consider and many people to talk to. The first of which was the school. We set up an appointment to meet with the principal and see if we could come up with a plan for the rest of Jordan's grade eight year.

It was a Wednesday afternoon and the principal, Mr. Burnell greeted us warmly and we sat down behind closed doors to talk about all that had led us to this point. We explained that Jordan would be beginning the process of transitioning and that we would be grateful for the school's support. We explained how Jordan would like to start coming to school dressing male and how we would like the teachers to begin to use male pronouns when addressing him. There was no resistance. Mr. Burnell swung into gear.

There was a Professional Development Day scheduled for that Friday which meant the students would not be in school but it was a mandatory day for the teachers. Mr. Burnell made special arrangements to have professionals come in and address the teachers on the topic of transgenderism and answer any questions they had on the topic. The teachers were told on Friday that when Jordan returned to school after the weekend they should begin addressing him with male pronouns.

Arrangements were made for Jordan to use any of the staff washrooms throughout the school so as not to upset him or any of the other students. It was an elementary school after all, grades kindergarten through eight, so there were some young students. We appreciated that these arrangements were being made for Jordan. There are transgender children who prefer to use the student washroom which they identify with. However, because Jordan had come out part way through the school year, the staff washrooms seemed like a fair solution and Jordan was comfortable with it. Washroom use is a topic all on its own and for this reason I have devoted an entire chapter to it later in this book.

In addition to addressing the subject with the school faculty on the Friday, Mr. Burnell suggested that Jordan stay home on Monday morning in order to allow him and the grade eight teachers an opportunity to address their students. Mr. Burnell felt, and we agreed, that it was important to prepare the grade eight students with whom Jordan shared classes as to the new development. Expectations could be set and the students could ask any questions they needed to without worry of Jordan being in the classroom at that time. In the previous week, Jordan had already confided in a couple of his closest friends that he was transgender and would likely be coming out to the school soon. That same week I received a call from a teacher at the school who wanted me to know Jordan had been spreading a rumour to a few of his classmates that he was transgender. I didn't offer an explanation to the teacher as I figured it would be forthcoming once an appointment with the principal could be arranged. I did say I appreciated her letting me know.

Before we left the principal's office that Wednesday Mr. Burnell also offered another suggestion to Jordan. He suggested that he could make a notebook available in his office that he would leave out in a specific place for Jordan. The idea was that this notebook could be used to pass private communications back and forth between himself and Jordan. Should there be anything at all that Jordan felt uncomfortable with or any issues that Jordan wanted to share; all he would need to do was write those things down and leave the notebook in Mr. Burnell's office. Mr. Burnell would then respond in writing in the notebook to Jordan and leave it for Jordan to retrieve the next day. What a thoughtful and considerate idea! Mr. Burnell was a true blessing to us.

Jordan's doctor had explained to us that Jordan's voice could drop in as soon as four weeks and once his voice dropped there would be no way to reverse that. Before that happened there were people that we needed to address, starting with the family that had entrusted Jordan with the care of their son, Trevor. Jordan had been babysitting Trevor after school and occasionally on weekends for over a year and a half. Trevor, for us was a blessing. Even though Jordan had been quite depressed during the time he had been babysitting Trevor, he always seemed to shake it off whenever Trevor was around. I know when Jordan was in a dark place he would often think about Trevor and how he would feel if anything were to happen to him. Trevor relied on Jordan. He looked up to him. That gave purpose and responsibility to Jordan that I believe has helped to strengthen Jordan's character and build his confidence.

It was only fair to give Trevor's parents as much notice as possible about Jordan's situation. Perhaps they would not want Jordan to continue to babysit for them. If that was the case, we wanted to ensure they had enough time to make alternative arrangements before Jordan's voice changed and explaining it all to their son would become more complicated.

We decided it was best for me to sit down with Trevor's mom, Ashley and explain things. Jordan and I had already discussed the different ways this could play out. We both agreed that we would not push them in any way should they feel it best to terminate their babysitting agreement with Jordan. Trevor was only six at the time and we had no idea what their reaction would be. Jordan had been babysitting Trevor for less than two years at the time and they had never known Jordon to have anything other than a female gender expression.

I set up a time early Saturday morning to go over and speak with Ashley. We sat on her living room sofa and I started right back at the beginning. I explained how growing up Jordan was a huge tomboy and always gravitated to doing the kinds of things little boys enjoyed doing. I went on to explain how Jordan had tried very hard to be more of a girl after puberty hit but instead of embracing the change he fell into a depressed state. I didn't provide all the details of that dark time but I did say the long and the short of it all is that we have discovered Jordan is transgender. I asked her if she knew what that meant and she replied she did. The conversation, though emotional at times, went smoothly from that point. I explained how Jordan would be getting a new hair cut almost immediately and dressing more male but that no other physical changes would be happening for at least a month. We wanted to give her and her husband time to digest this news. If they felt, for whatever reason, they did not want to have to explain this to their son, or that they no longer wanted Jordan looking after him they would have the time to find another sitter. She appreciated that.

She asked me questions, many the same ones my husband and I had ourselves asked the doctors. She wanted to know if

Jordan's mood would change because of the drugs he was on, an obvious concern she would have. I told her we would be keeping an eye out for any such changes but were told neither medication should have any negative effects on Jordan's personality. I explained that he would be keeping his first name. He was fortunate that the name Jordan was not gender specific. That would make it easier for her son should she decide to continue to engage Jordan as a sitter. I did say that after a time we would want her son to try to address Jordan using male pronouns. For this reason, and the appearance changes coming down the road, explaining transgenderism to her child was something she would need to consider. I left it in her hands and told her to take as much time as she needed to think things over and discuss it with her husband. Together, whatever they decided would be respected by our family.

I have to tell you, this was one of the first really powerful demonstrations of love I saw on this journey. As soon as I left their house, her husband pulled into their driveway and it wasn't thirty minutes later that they were both at our door asking to speak to Jordan. My fingers and my toes were crossed that this was going to be good news. Jordan came to the door and they said to him: "Trevor loves you and we love how you care so well for him. We never ever worry when he is in your care and he is really happy to come here. Of course, we still want you to babysit Trevor. We fully support you and are very grateful our son has you in his life." Listening, it was hard for me to hold back the tears. We received the good news we had hoped for. I was so happy for their expression of love towards Jordan. This was the first of many blessings we were to receive.

That weekend, Jordan cut his hair very short and was ready to sport a whole new look when he returned to school Monday afternoon. Mariah was still struggling with the whole idea of her sister becoming her brother and we were trying to respect her by giving her time to adjust and not over stimulating her with the daily updates on Jordan's situation. I was pleasantly surprised when she decided to accompany us to the salon that Saturday and she even offered an opinion on the new hair cut that Jordan had chosen. I was very proud of Mariah that day for stepping up and being there for Jordan because, for Jordan, this hair cut represented so much more than just a new hair style. Jordan was excited to cut his hair and start dressing in male clothes again. For him, this was a new beginning. He made the decision to donate his hair to an organization that makes wigs for woman cancer patients who have lost their hair through chemotherapy and other treatments. Looking in the mirror that afternoon I believe Jordan recognized himself for the first time in almost two years. He appeared very pleased with his new haircut.

Jordan has a great face, beautiful as a girl, handsome as a guy but we could not take it for granted that this would always be the case. It was another reason to not delay transition. Facial features become more gender dominant through puberty and transitioning earlier means one's face is more convincing as the transitioned gender. My heart goes out to those that transition late in life, especially those that are going from male to female. It can be difficult for some to pull off the desired look, commonly understood in the transgender community as "passing" for their respective gender. That seems like such a negative term "passing" as if they aren't really who they are, but rather masquerading as something they aren't. Fortunately for Jordan, this was not going to be an issue, with a change in wardrobe and a new haircut Jordan went from female to male overnight. Jordan was in high spirits as the weekend came to a close. It had been a great couple of days for him and he was ready to get back to school and see his friends.

Jim dropped Jordan off at school during lunch on Monday like Principal Burnell had requested we do. Jim told me that he saw Jordan's friends waiting just inside the main doors to the school. He said they greeted Jordan warmly with big smiles on their faces. After dropping Jordan off Jim returned home and he and I waited for the afternoon to end so we could hear how the teachers and students handled Jordan's new look and the news of him being transgender. According to Jordan it went very well. The teachers used male pronouns from that very first afternoon and the kids were, or at least seemed to be, very supportive. A week or so later I asked Mr. Burnell if he had gotten any calls from parents with concerns. I was surprised to learn the school only received a couple of calls and Mr. Burnell assured me they were easily handled and I had nothing to worry about. A hundred people can tell you not to worry, but as a parent you still do. I worried that Jordan would get bullied or beat up or treated poorly in some way by students that either didn't understand or didn't agree with or approve of Jordan's transition.

One of the early stories Jordan shared with me about happenings at school was about gym class. Now that he was attending school as a male student, he could not very well enter the girls change room and somehow entering the boys change room still seemed uncomfortable both for him and the other male students. So, again, the school stepped up and provided a private place for Jordan to change. Later that day one of Jordan's female classmates told him it was so strange being in the girls change room listening to the other girls talk about him. They were saying things like: "Wow, Jordan's hot as a guy." Jordan said he and his friend laughed about it.

Things calmed down quickly and everyone just settled back into their usual routines. I think most of his friends thought he was very brave and cool to stand up for himself and make the transition. Many understood it was not the life he would have chosen for himself, just a life he knew he had to live. Jordan was fortunate to be born when he was and not twenty years earlier. Back then, I don't think classmates would have been so accepting.

As we got closer to the end of the school year, I began to worry about what high school Jordan should attend. Jordan worried too. There were really only two schools in our area, one a public school where likely seventy five percent of his grade eight classmates would be going and a Catholic School. I didn't think the Catholic School would be the best choice for a transgender student and Jordan would have liked nothing more than to be able to enter high school just like any other regular guy. He felt attending the school seventy five percent of his classmates were going to attend was not a great choice either. I wondered where he could go where his past didn't follow him and where people would just see him as himself. I prayed again asking God to please give me some direction as to which school would be the best for Jordan.

Not too much time passed when I received an unexpected call from Mr. Burnell asking me if Jim and I could come into the school. I asked him if everything was okay and he quickly assured me that it was. Jordan was already at school but Mr. Burnell wanted to sit down with all three of us. Once we were all seated in his office, he asked us if we had given any thought as to where we would register Jordan for high school in September. I explained how we weren't terribly happy with our choices and that I had been feeling distraught about it. He said he wanted to offer us another option, a third option. I could not imagine what that would be.

Mr. Burnell told us about a friend of his who was the principal at a school just outside our area. He said that, if we wanted, they would work with the school board to get approval for an out of area transfer for Jordan. He felt this high school would be a good fit. If approved, it would mean Jordan could attend a school that none of the students from his current school would be attending. If this worked out he truly would be able to enter high school as himself. It was explained to us that this out of area principal was willing to ensure his past did not interfere with his high school experience and that we could register Jordan as a male student from the get go.

We were told that the teachers and staff at this high school didn't even need to be made aware that Jordan was a transgender student. I wondered about school transcripts and things of that nature because Jordan was registered in school as Jordan Catherine. Mr. Burnell said he was sure he could get all the records changed to reflect only a middle initial of C on all school papers and that all school records prior to Jordan entering high school would be sealed at the board level. This would mean teachers at the high school would not have access to Jordan's earlier report cards or transcripts. Was this really happening? It felt as if doors were being opened to Jordan that we never even knew existed. We were even offered a guided tour of the school before making a decision. We jumped at the chance.

The following week, Jim and I toured this out of area high

school with Jordan and had a meeting with the principal there who was helping to make all this possible. Jordan loved the school and we all liked the principal. The school board granted the transfer under special recommendation from Mr. Burnell and the high school principal where he would be attending in September. It was settled. Jordan would attend a school just out of our area. It meant some logistics on our end, given it was about a twenty minute drive two times a day to get Jordan to and from school, but it was sure to be worth it.

Jordan finished out his grade eight year, and graduated with honours! I'm so proud of my son for keeping up his grades through all of this. If you are wondering about his physical and emotional self, I can tell you both were getting stronger. His health continued to make progress, week by week, month by month through the end of that school year. At this point Jordan had been on testosterone for more than six months. With each additional month that passed I saw more and more of the vibrant person Jordan once was. Now when his friends came to the door he didn't have us turn them away. Instead he greeted them warmly and enjoyed hanging out with them again. We literally saw that Jordan's face was lighting up again, his confidence was returning and we knew without a doubt that we were on the right path.

Then there was my personal promise to Jordan. I promised not to tell. While we were trying to navigate our family's new reality, Jordan made it clear to me that he just wanted to have an attention free transition. Being a public activist or role model was not on his agenda. He had no interest in being out to the world but rather expressed his desire to just be known as a regular teenage boy. There was no question in my mind that this was very important to him so, I promised I would do my part to help protect his privacy. This meant promising to not unnecessarily discuss the fact that he was transgender with new people that would come into our life. This helped to keep me on my toes. It was challenging in the beginning and took longer than I would have liked to fully adjust to the male pronouns. I didn't want to slip up but it was easy to do. In the past, when dinner was ready, I used to always call out "girls dinner is ready" now I call out "kids dinner's ready." It sounds so simple but when you do something one way, referred to someone one way for so long, it takes time. Jordan was patient with us and I think it helped him to know we were trying and would quickly correct ourselves or apologize when we slipped up.

New people that entered our lives were not told of Jordan's past. First, because it wasn't necessary for them to know and second, by not telling them, I was respecting my son's wishes. Just like anyone else, he had a right to decide for himself how, if and when he shared his history with others. His gender dysphoria seemed better when he wasn't being reminded regularly of his past. He was happy being treated as he wished to be treated, just like a regular guy. Jordan's health and happiness are what matter to me, so making and honouring this promise to him was easy.

As a parent, even though I saw this great improvement in Jordan, part of me could not help but be a little sad for the daughter that had been left behind. Jordan was the same person, yet he wasn't. When you have a child, it is natural to have certain ideas of how you would see their life play out. You envision things they might do, and the relationship you expect to have with that child as they grow older. What was happening with Jordan was not the path I expected, the one I had seen playing out in my mind. I saw a much easier life for my child, one without gender identity struggles and the pain that comes along with that. I pictured sharing mother-daughter times not mother-son times and that was an adjustment. It wasn't that it was any worse or any better than what I expected. It was only different. It was like having to rethink your family dynamics, how we interact with each other. I just wanted Jordan to have a simple life. I love both my children equally and support them both wholeheartedly and I think they know that. Jordan may not have the simple life I envisioned for him, but his life is far simpler than it would have been if he chose not to live his life as his authentic self.

CHAPTER 10

Maybe She is Gay?

It is hard enough to worry about your core family, how they are reacting and coping with the change but there are also others in the extended family that can be affected. While I believe one's core family should always take high priority, the reactions of extended family members can also have a huge impact, either positively or negatively on the situation. This impact grows or lessens based on how your family's lives are intertwined with theirs.

Jordan was old enough to approach the subject matter himself and wanted to be the one that approached the topic with much of our extended family, beginning with his grandparents. Jim's parents had passed away, so there was only one set of grandparents for Jordan to approach. You never know how an older generation will react. Will they even know what transgenderism is? Will they be able to accept this, accept Jordan? The thing in our family was that my parents were always very close to my children growing up. They saw first hand the differences in our kids and loved them both for their individuality as much as we did. They also saw the drastic change in Jordan during the two years leading up to this point and were all too aware of the radical change in Jordan's personality. They saw how dark and withdrawn Jordan had become and were very concerned at the time, knowing something was very wrong. For them, it was a great relief that Jordan was able to come out from that darkness.

I remember them saying to me that they always felt Jordan was more than just a regular tomboy. Like myself, the possibility of him being a transgender child was not on their radar nor did they know much, if anything about it. They received the news with open hearts and arms and then began their own journey of searching for knowledge so they too could better understand their transgender grandchild. Never for a second, was there anything but genuine love and compassion for Jordan, our family and the journey we were about to embark on. Jordan's grandparents were quick to pick up the new pronouns and see him as their grandson rather than their granddaughter.

The next of our extended family to be told were Jordan's Uncle Terry, his Aunt Cathy, their son Robert and his fiancée Cindy who were all visiting for the weekend. Jordan bravely addressed them all at once beginning by asking the simple question "Do you know what transgender means?" Now, these were not some distant relatives that you only see once every few years. Terry and Cathy are Jordan's godparents and our families are close. They witnessed, like his grandparents did, the strong boyish tendencies Jordan had expressed since early childhood. Even though this may have made understanding things a bit easier I think they were still taken back a bit. Upon hearing the news, they all offered loving support to Jordan and accepted what he was telling them without question, at least that is how it was to Jordan. In private, Jordan's aunt and uncle expressed their own concerns to me. Did I really think Jordan was old enough to be making such a permanent life changing decision? Should we not wait until Jordan was older and would know for sure what sexual orientation he might have? Maybe Jordan is gay, not transgender.

There it was; the biggest misconception about transgenderism. I explained how gender and sexual orientation are completely separate things. I assured them we had done our research. It does not help clear up this common misconception about transgender people when transgender is lumped in with the sexual orientation terms by way of the LGBT (Lesbian, Gay, Bi-Sexual Transgender) communities or groups. The first three LGB (Lesbian, Gay and Bi-Sexual) all refer to ones sexual orientation and explain who one is attracted to romantically or sexually. However, those individuals represented by the T (Transgender) are simply persons who have a physical or biological gender that does not match up with their mental gender. It is a gender identity issue, not a sexual orientation issue.

In Jordan's case, while born into a physical female body, his brain has always believed himself to be male. Gender is one thing, it is who we are; sexual orientation is completely secondary and separate from gender identity. A transgender person could still be lesbian, gay or bi-sexual but a transgender person can just as easily see themselves as heterosexual. For Jordan to be attracted to females would mean Jordan is a heterosexual male, not a female attracted to other females (lesbian). A transgender person like Jordan is a person born in the biological sex opposite to that with which they self identify.

Now, back to our extended family; Jordan had me discuss it with other aunts and uncles that he didn't see as often, as well as with a few of our closer cousins. For the most part, this went very well with everyone accepting Jordan's news and supporting his new gender identity.

There is one funny story I will share with you. One of Jordan's aunts, whom we do not see very often, found out about Jordan from his uncle. After she had been told, we learned that she had had a rather strong reaction to the news. I guess she was not one to believe transgenderism was real, but rather something that could be "fixed". She went on to share her thoughts with her own parents, expecting them to fully support her position. Had they supported her, I would not have been the least bit surprised because they are from a much older generation. What actually happened was quite comical. She went to her parents and basically explained the decisions my husband and I were making to assist Jordan in transitioning. She remarked that it was crazy. Her parents looked at her very seriously and said: "Oh no, you're wrong, transgender IS a real thing, we know because we saw it on Jerry Springer." LOL, how great is that! That little anecdote was just what I need to hear. My mood had been so serious since all this started. It felt good to laugh out loud.

You can argue over the merits of a media personality like Jerry Springer being the source of information on this subject, but at least in discussing it, he opened their eyes to it. As parents of a transgender child, Jim and I are thankful to the media for shining light on the topic. I am not a rah, rah person and my son certainly is not, nor as I have already mentioned, does he want to live a public life being out to the world, but we are grateful to those individuals that are. Without people like Jerry Springer, Chaz Bono, Janet Mock or Caitlyn Jenner, we wouldn't know as much as we do about transgender people. Television shows like 'I am Cait' or 'Transparent' also bring transgender people into the foreground. Individuals like Chaz Bono have helped to educate the world like few can. 'Becoming Chaz' was one of the first documentaries Jim and I watched after discovering Jordan was transgender.

There are people like my son that do not really associate themselves with the term transgender. Jordan thinks of himself just as a young man, nothing more, and nothing less. In fact, later in the chapter entitled New Identification: Challenging the Bureaucracy, I will share with you a letter Jordan wrote advocating for himself as just a regular teenage boy.

I firmly believe that the ability of our extended family to accept Jordan for who he is and to not waiver in their love and support for him has made things so much easier. Acceptance is huge for anyone, but for a transgender person, emotional support can have a tremendous impact. If I am aware of someone with non-accepting views or strong opposing positions on transgender people, I will definitely do my best, as a mom, to keep that person or persons at a distance from my son. Instead I work to surround him with those that are understanding, compassionate and accepting. Fortunately for us, there are a rare few in our life that are not supportive of Jordan. Those rare few are people who really do not play a large part in Jordan's life anyway, people whom we may see only once every couple of years. So, it's quite easy to avoid situations where Jordan might come in contact with these people.

I still worry a great deal about Mariah because I know there are several people close to her that are not supportive of transgender people in general. Some may be aware of Jordan's history and others may not. For me, it is a consistent worry that those individuals may use their influence on Mariah and bring undo pain, confusion and heartache to her. They may damage the bond between my children and even our core family. While this may not be their intent, it may be the result. Judgement is a terrible thing. When good, honest people lay judgement on others sometimes it can be hard to separate judgement from wisdom, especially when you are still young.

Mariah is an incredible young woman, loved and respected by many. She has a loving heart and a good head on her shoulders. As her mom, I find it incredibly difficult sometimes to stand back and just let Mariah discover things for herself. Sometimes, I feel like so many people want a piece of her or are trying to use their influence on her to pull her in one direction or another. I hold onto the faith I have in her, that she does know right from wrong, will recognize wisdom when it comes her way and spot judgement when it is right in front of her. I pray that her own life experiences will help guide her and support her on her path. I don't feel that she will ever know just how much I love her (although I tell her almost daily), how very proud I am of her and how I so desperately just want her to be happy.

PART THREE

A Journey of Self Discovery

CHAPTER 11

Why am I Transgender?

What causes one to be transgender is a question asked by many but answered by few. Those that have tackled this question, even on a deeply scientific level, have had their findings debated and challenged. Ultimately, I have never heard an absolute answer to this question. I have, however, heard many theories. It is the same nature vs. nurture argument people have been having for decades. If transgender people are born that way, the cause is based in nature. Conversely, the nurture theory is that one's gender identity is a result of their upbringing or parenting. For example, in the case of an intersexed baby (one born with what appears to be both sets of genitalia) a decision is made by the parents at birth as to the sex of the child and they proceed to raise the child based on that choice. There are documented cases where a child, whose parents made the decision of gender, later grow convinced they are in the wrong body and desperately desire to change their gender. This suggests that parenting and environment actually have little to nothing to do with a person's gender identity.

Doctors and scientists alike seem to support the nature theory. Linking transgenderism to genetics or brain function or brain structure suggesting it is predetermined before birth. Some believe prenatal androgen exposure in the womb directly affects gender identity. What specifically occurs during the early stages of cellular development is unclear, or at the very least, debatable among scientists. However, they do all seem to share the common belief that gender dysphoria is rooted in nature. It is not a choice that transgender people make nor is it a result of their surroundings.

I once heard a theory about a mother who was pregnant with opposite sex twins. The theory is that if one twin dies in the womb and the fetus of the deceased twin is absorbed by the mother's body somehow residual traces of their gender can be passed onto the surviving twin.

While it is interesting to examine all the different nature theories, it doesn't get us any closer to an irrefutable answer today. Though, I do suspect science is getting closer.

Here's a question to ponder. When does the spirit enter the body? If we are in fact spiritual beings, it is interesting to think about when the spirit and our fetus actually connect. Perhaps our spiritual self understands our gender to be preordained by God before our incarnation into this world. If this is the case, we could, before we are even born, have knowledge about our own gender. If this is true, it stands to reason that no one outside of ourselves could convince us we are anything other than that which we believe we are. As interesting as this theory is, that's all it is, another theory. We can't prove it or disprove it. It can, however, give us pause to think about the great unknowns in this universe. It seems fair to acknowledge that as much as we think we have life figured out, it is possible we have not figured out much at all.

Searching for a cause or a reason is pointless and can only cause more pain. There is still more for science to uncover. Looking for the answer to why could literally drive you crazy. As a parent, do we really need to know why our child is transgender? Do we need to know exactly what happened during the gestational period? Sure, it would be wonderful to have a tidy little answer for all the cynics, but honestly, if you are searching desperately for an answer, ask yourself, why are you searching for that answer? While the answer may bring some personal comfort, it's not going to change the outcome. Jordan doesn't seem concerned with the why. He has had plenty of opportunities to ask his doctors this question yet he never has. He just accepts himself for who his is. He likely realizes, it doesn't really matter, knowing why won't change anything.

The gender incongruity felt by a transgender person can usually be traced back to a very young age. I have memories of putting Jordan in dresses at a young age and him tearing them off, insisting he would not wear them. I remember the struggle with a very strong willed child. I recall my attempts at compromise, like giving in and allowing Jordan to cut and keep his hair very short if he pierced his ears (something I mentioned earlier I regret). It became increasingly difficult to encourage Jordan to dress like a girl or take up any activities he construed as feminine. In the end, while some may judge me as not having tried hard enough, I know there is little a person can do to change the will of another person. No matter what I did as a parent to encourage female behaviour, Jordan was going to have no part of it.

If believing in any particular theory, even one of your own, brings you comfort then I say, great, hold onto that. Just understand that science isn't there yet to provide us with a neat and tidy explanation and I don't believe having one is necessary to moving forward. Moving forward could look different for different people. It could be getting to a place where you are ready to help your child. Moving forward could be getting counselling for you and your child so you can both get the support you need. It could mean getting educated on the topic, and by reading this book it is my hope that you are off to a great start. Whatever moving forward represents for you, the important thing is, it's moving forward not backwards and that is a great first step.

CHAPTER 12

Mental Health

If you have a friend or loved one who is struggling with their gender identity you may have already been told by someone that gender dysphoria is a mental illness. Gender dysphoria may be the name given to explain the conflict a transgender person feels, but that doesn't mean they were not born that way. The fact their gender identity does not align with their biological sex does not, in my opinion, warrant classifying them as mentally ill. The medical world is slow to acknowledging this and while their labelling of transgender people needs to change, in my opinion, it's not likely to happen over night.

It is hard to discuss mental health, especially in Canada, without thinking of CAMH. CAMH stands for The Centre for Addiction and Mental Health, based in Toronto, Ontario. Regardless of where you stand on believing gender dysphoria is a mental health issue this organization can be a source of valuable information, support and possibly even care. According to their own website, CAMH is recognized as a leading research center worldwide and is also Canada's largest mental health and addiction teaching hospital. CAMH claims they are affiliated with the

University of Toronto, and that they are a Pan American Health Organization/World Health Organization Collaborating Centre.

Jim and I did consult with CAMH. We carefully reviewed papers they had written on the subject of gender dysphoria and spoke to medical professionals there. They offer both inpatient and outpatient therapies to transgender individuals. They take the idea of transitioning, especially where hormone therapies and surgeries are concerned, very seriously and rightly so. While we do not live in the Toronto area, we did consider CAMH as an option available to us. However, after careful research we decided it was not in Jordan's best interest to attend CAMH for any consultations or therapy. I'll explain this decision in a moment, but first let me say, that what is right for one individual is not necessarily what is right for another. It is essential to do your own research. If you are the parent of a gender questioning or transgender child you will want to source out any and all channels of support available to you. Then you can decide on the course of action that is best suited for your child.

We decided against CAMH for Jordan for a couple of reasons, none of which, at the time, were a lack of confidence in the medical professionals there. The main consideration for us was Jordan's age and the fact that Jordan had already begun puberty. CAMH has, or had at the time, a strict policy that a transgender person must be under their care for a minimum of two years before hormone therapy could be considered. They wanted to ensure that the individual was living their life in the gender they identified with both in private and public for those two years. Jordan was just coming out of a period of time where he was trying desperately to be a girl, but had otherwise already been living male for the better part of his life. If we were to go the CAMH route, Jordan would be forced to wait two more years before hormone blockers could be used. During this time, Jordan would continue to develop as a female making his female traits more dominant and more difficult to reverse later. CAMH would have offered therapy sessions to Jordan every other week for this two year period. The other option we had was to have Jordan continue on with the therapist he currently had and with whom we had already developed a good relationship.

Transgender people, who seek therapy through CAMH for a minimum of two years, pass all their psychological tests and meet their behavioural requirements can be put on the path to hormonal transition and surgical transition if desired. Those that are put on the path to transition through CAMH may have financial benefits available to them.

Some provinces' health plans in Canada, like Ontario, only allow certain transgender surgeries to be covered by their health plans if the transgender diagnosis comes from CAMH. For female to male top surgery, this coverage is about fifty percent. While this represents a large savings, it was not worth holding Jordan hostage for two more years. We decided to continue with those medical professionals we had already started with which included his family doctor, his therapist and his endocrinologist. I learned from others that the therapies at CAMH where incredibly intense. I didn't feel it was necessary to expose Jordan to that type of psychological stress when the medical professionals in Jordan's life had already concluded a definite transgender diagnosis. We wanted Jordan to get help without being subjected to more tests and felt going the CAMH route would only prolong his suffering. Your situation may be different so, again, I suggest you do your own research and become as knowledgeable as you can on the subject. Greater knowledge should lead to a deeper understanding, so you can be better equipped to make an informed decision.

CAMH update: Just prior to publishing this book I have learned that the Youth Gender Identity Clinic at CAMH was closed. It appears they are still providing care to persons over the age of eighteen, but that there is currently no treatment available for children and teens. This is not to say it will not reopen in the future. For our personal situation, my further research reaffirms to me that, Jim and I made the correct decision to not involve CAMH in Jordan's care. At the time we were considering CAMH, I had been told by parents of other transgender children attending the clinic that the psychological methods of the clinic seemed intense. One mother told me that her child came out more conflicted and confused about their gender identity than when they went in.

My recent research suggests that the clinic had been engaging in reparative treatments that would try to force the gender questioning youth to conform to their sexual gender assigned at birth. It is my understanding that their clinic head, Dr. Kenneth Zucker, has been relieved of his duties. Dr. Kenneth Zucker is a psychologist who was head of the CAMH gender identity clinic for decades.

There are others who support Dr. Zucker and his methods. Hundreds of his peers from around the globe signed a petition in support of him and protesting his removal from the CAMH Gender Identity Clinic.

For me, in the end, I am glad we found the doctors we did for Jordan because he has had nothing but exceptional care. Perhaps our decision to not go the CAMH route proved to be even wiser than we had originally thought it to be.

I suspect that at some point, the American Psychiatric Association (APA) will delist transgenderism as a mental illness from their DSM (Diagnostic and Statistical Manual). They de-listed homosexuality back in 1974. If the APA does delist transgenderism hopefully the World Health Organization will respond similarly. I hope that I will see this happen during my lifetime.

London's Independent headline reads: "Denmark will become first country to no longer define being transgender as a mental illness" as reported on May 14, 2016. The article went on to say that "Government Officials said classifying transgender people as mentally ill was "stigmatising" and they had "run out of patience" with the World Health Organization's (WHO) work on the same definition." According to the article, plans are set for Danish officials to move on the change themselves on January 1, 2017. It appears Denmark will proceed regardless of whether the WHO changes their official position.

CHAPTER 13

Steps in Transitioning

A person's transition is as unique and individual as they are. Each transgender person decides what transition means for them and proceeds accordingly. The first steps for Jordan began when he cut his hair and reverted back to the male gender expression he had when he was younger. The next was when he began his hormone replacement therapy. As I mentioned earlier, Jordan's endocrinologist put him on two medications. One was to stop the female hormone (estrogen) and the other was to introduce the male hormone (testosterone). While testosterone is a natural hormone, the drug which Jordan was inhaling twice daily to stop estrogen is a synthetic drug. It is not clear what, if any, the long term side effects of being on this drug might be. Stopping the drug during transition is not an option. As soon as the drug is stopped, the female hormones would kick back in. Breasts would restart development and menstruation could start up again. Not to mention the hormone war it would start in the body with both female and male hormones fighting for domination. The only way Jordan can stop the hormone nasal blockers is to have a hysterectomy, so this was on the table for discussion later.

As part of maintaining Jordan's health, his blood is drawn and monitored regularly by his doctors to ensure everything is within normal range. His tests have always come back fine. That is, with the exception of one blood test taken not long after he started on hormone therapy. That particular test came back showing he had an unusually high hemoglobin level. This means the level of blood inside his body was too high. His doctor asked if Jordan snored and if he took naps during the day. I replied yes to both. He definitely snored and often would take a nap between school and dinner time. His family doctor wanted him to see a specialist to rule out sleep apnea. The specialist Jordan saw wanted to have him spend a night at a sleep clinic so they could monitor his sleeping behaviour and see if sleep apnea could actually be the cause of his high hemoglobin levels.

Jordan obliged and spent one night at the sleep clinic hooked up to so many monitors he looked like an alien from outer space. It took a while for us to get the results, but it turned out he did not have sleep apnea. We needed to look for what else might be the cause. Jordan's doctor asked about the amount of fluid Jordan had been drinking and I said I thought it was much less than it should be. I know at that time Jordan was uncomfortable about using washrooms outside of home and he likely drank less so he could avoid this situation. I know one of the first things he would do when he got home from school was use the washroom. Jordan was not alone on this. The anxiety and distress transgender people feel around washroom use is very real. Once Jordan overcame this discomfort and began to drink more, his hemoglobin level returned to normal.

Another area of discomfort for Jordan were the binders he had been wearing to bind his chest during the early part of his transition. They were often uncomfortable and he found them quite restrictive, especially after a meal. Sometimes he would even say it was difficult to breathe. They also held moisture in which made Jordan more susceptible to back acne. Jordan hated wearing them, but felt they were a necessary evil. Jordan's first priority was his chest. What he really wanted was chest surgery.

It was during the summer after he had started the hormone blockers and testosterone, approximately eight months into his transition when we decided to consult with a surgeon. At that time Jordan was still fourteen and the surgeon we were going to consult with had never performed this surgery on anyone as young as Jordan. This particular surgeon, Dr. McLean, was well known in North America for having performed many transgender top surgeries and his credentials, experience and list of many happy clients is what drew us to him. Jordan had been through many psychological tests by various medical professionals and was doing well at this point in his transition. The surgeon still wanted to meet and speak with not just my husband and me, but also with Jordan about why he felt this surgery was necessary.

There are transgender people who feel perfectly comfortable never going under the knife, deciding to bind instead, but this was not where Jordan stood on the matter. Jordan felt a very strong need to have the surgery in order to feel whole and right in his body. The surgery itself was a chest masculinisation (double mastectomy). What this means is in addition to removing Jordan's breasts, the surgeon would carefully shape the tissue to create a natural male looking chest. It is a day surgery done in a private clinic much like a hospital setting. Depending on breast size there are two different types of surgery available. One consists of making a half circular incision under each breast and removing breast tissue. The nipples may need to be removed and repositioned or cut down in size depending on how large they are to begin with.

The second type of chest surgery, which is only available to those with very small breasts, is called keyhole surgery. Keyhole surgery makes tiny incisions around the bottom of the areola, lifting the areola, with nipple still attached, up out of the way. The breast tissue is then carefully removed by scalpel and the areola with nipple is reattached. Keyhole surgery leaves far less scarring but surgeons will try to minimize scarring when keyhole is not possible by making the larger incisions along what will become the peck line of the patient's new male chest. If the person has a hairy chest this will certainly serve to hide the scars and there are also some creams available that may help lighten the appearance of the scars.

After the initial consultation, evaluation, and examination of Jordan by the surgeon, he agreed to do the surgery. Jordan would be the youngest transgender patient this surgeon had ever agreed to operate on (by about two years). Jordan was very excited and my husband and I were so happy for him.

Next we were sent in to meet with the administrator who booked all of the appointments and were hoping for something over Christmas break. We knew the surgeon was booked up months ahead and we were hoping by setting it up in the summer we might be able to schedule the surgery over Jordan's two week Christmas break. The recovery time could easily be two weeks and if we could schedule it over the school holiday, Jordan's studies would not be impacted. As it was they were quite booked up, but they had had a cancellation for the following month of August about two weeks before school was scheduled to start up again. We were offered that appointment.

Now, you have to understand we didn't go into that office thinking it could happen that soon and we were not prepared to be presented with that possibility. We hadn't planned it this way and were definitely caught off guard. The surgery would cost about eight thousand dollars when it was all said and done and we had thought we would still have months to save for that. The administrator said: "You can have August 20th if you want it. We just received a cancellation and that rarely happens, but you would need to put down half of the cost today to hold that date. The balance would be due on the day of the surgery." My husband and I looked at each other then looked at Jordan whose eyes told us how excited he was at this possibility.

We asked the administrator to step outside for just a minute so we could discuss this in private. My husband and I began to think about how we would come up with all this money in the next thirty days. Both of us are very averse to debt, but in the end, we only had to look at each other and without saying a word we knew we would find a way.

The administrator came back into the room and took her seat behind her desk and asked us if we had made a decision. I said we decided to move ahead with the surgery on August 20th and my husband handed her his credit card for the deposit. At that very moment Jordan got up out of his chair, walked over to his Dad, gave him a big hug and said a very audible, "Thank You!" With that the administrator started to cry. Nodding her head she pushed the papers we were to sign forward towards us on the desk. It was a very emotional exchange. My husband and I looked at each other again and just knew it would all work out, we didn't need to speak a word.

Over the next thirty days there was a lot to do. Jordan had to have a physical with his regular doctor and blood work done. Requisition forms and pre-surgery forms had to be filled out and sent to Jordan's family doctor and then onto the surgeon. There was travel and a hotel stay to arrange as we were from out of town. There was a pre-op visit with the surgeon to explain more details about the actual day, which offered Jordan and us an opportunity to discuss any additional questions or concerns we had.

I can recall conversations I had with Jordan about the upcoming surgery and asking him "Aren't you nervous about the operation or worried about the results?" He replied: "You are the only one doing the worrying." He was completely at peace with it and knew everything would go smoothly. How could he know that? He just had this total assurance about it. We had discussed all the possible things that could go wrong; the possible complications during surgery and after but still Jordan shrugged his shoulders saying, "I'm not worried at all." He had a great faith about everything, and I so admired him for that.

Before we knew it the month had passed. Jim, Jordan and I packed our overnight bags and made the trip back into the Greater Toronto Area (GTA) for the big day. The staff at the clinic greeted us warmly as soon as we arrived. There was some last minute paperwork to take care of which didn't take more than a few minutes to complete. Soon after, they got Jordan settled in a private room. The anaesthesiologist came in to introduce himself to Jordan and see how he was doing. Shortly after that the surgeon, Dr. McLean came in to visit with us. He too wanted to see how Jordan was doing and asked him if he had any last minute questions. Jordan had none. He was just looking forward to getting things underway. Once Jordan was all prepped for surgery and ready to be taken into the operating room Jim and I were told we should leave and come back in about four hours. So, reluctantly, we did. We stayed nearby with our cell phones both close at hand and tried not to worry. Anyone who has ever had a child in surgery for any reason knows the helpless feeling you have while you wait and hope everything is going smoothly.

After about three and a half hours Jim and I returned to the clinic in the hopes of getting some news. It wasn't long afterwards that we were told Jordan was out of surgery and that everything went very well. I was anxious to see him, but was told I had to wait. We were told there were other patients in the recovery area where Jordan was and for patient privacy reasons, they could not allow us back to see him. The nurses would come out to see us in the waiting room every fifteen minutes or so to reassure us Jordan was doing well. I'm certain they could tell how impatient I was getting. Had we been told ahead of time that there would be a time lapse between when he came out of surgery and when we could see him I may have been less jittery. Eventually, after what seemed like forever to me, we were allowed back and were able to see for ourselves that Jordan was doing well. He was still a little groggy from the general anaesthetic, but he laid there smiling feeling glad it was all done. That evening we stayed close by at a hotel just in case there were any complications during the night. Thankfully, there were none.

The next morning we went back to the clinic for a post-op visit with the surgeon and to have Jordan's bandages removed so he could see his chest for the first time. We were all delighted with the results. There was a bit of fluid built up on one side, so the surgeon inserted a needle and removed it. Jordan told us it wasn't painful having that done and that he hardly felt it. They re-dressed his chest and Jordan received clean bandages and special care instructions to take home.

When this surgery is performed, they leave two drains in that exit the body, one under each armpit. They put the drain incisions in the armpit area because even if there are tiny scars that remain, they will be covered by armpit hair. This is smart on the surgeon's part. The drain lines were about a foot to a foot and a half long and drained extra fluid from Jordan's chest into two plastic sacks. The drain lines clip onto the bandages just off to each side of the chest. For the next week or so these sacks needed to be emptied at regular intervals. At first they were emptied quite regularly, then as each day passed a little less often until there was hardly any more fluid draining from Jordan's chest at all.

Jordan was given some strong pain pills to help manage any pain or discomfort. He was only on those for the first couple of days. The worst of it was over and the pain in his chest began to subside. After that, most of the discomfort he was experiencing was coming from where the drains actually entered his body. Any pull or movement on the drain lines made him wince. He was only taking Advil as needed at this point. All in all Jordan was a trooper who smiled often and complained little about his discomfort. After about ten days post-op he no longer needed any pain management. He was extremely pleased with his new chest.

The next step was to take Jordan to his family doctor's office to have the drains removed. If we had lived in the Toronto area this would have been done at the clinic where his surgery was performed. He told me the sensation of having the drains pulled out felt very weird, but not painful, just a little irritating. Jordan's recovery went very well and when school was ready to start up again, the first week in September, Jordan was ready to go. The only thing the surgeon told Jordan he should be mindful of when returning to school, was to remember not to lift or carry anything heavy. He was advised to lift no more than five pounds for the first six weeks. That was a bit of a challenge if you've seen the backpacks kids carry these days.

It was the beginning of his first year in high school and Jordan was able to dress normally without having to ever wear a binder again. For Jordan, that was a very big deal. It was nice to see him enter high school looking and feeling like a regular teenage boy. He was so grateful to have his chest surgery behind him. It was a real blessing that he was able to attend a high school where no one knew him or his history. It wasn't long before he met some terrific new friends and was settling into his new school and classes.

Remember that big credit card bill we had racked up paying for Jordan's surgery? Well something crazy happened about six weeks after the surgery that I attribute only as a gift from God. My mom had asked me to attend a concert with her, someone she really wanted to see. This particular artist was not someone I thought I would enjoy and I honestly didn't want to go, but something told me I should. The concert was at a casino venue. We decided to make a mother daughter night of it. We went early to have dinner and booked a room in the hotel that was connected to casino so we could stay over after the show. We had a very nice dinner and enjoyed each others company. The concert itself wasn't all that bad and my mom really enjoyed herself so I was happy.

After the concert ended we decided we would do a little gambling before we went to our hotel room. I decided to play the penny slots for awhile. I was drawn to this group of six machines that were all laid out in a circle side by side. I sat down at one of the machines and began to play. It was a penny machine and the maximum bet was $1.50. This group of six machines were all the same. I started by putting a fifty dollar bill in the machine and began to play always selecting max bet. After a while I was up about one hundred and fifty dollars, not bad right? Well the strangest thing happened to me while I was sitting there playing. I had a very strong sense I should move one seat to my left. It was as if someone or something was saying "move left". Now partly because of my earlier experiences I thought to myself if this was a higher power talking to me, if this was God talking, I was going to listen. I pushed the cash out button on the machine and took my hundred and fifty dollar voucher and moved one machine to my left. I inserted the voucher and resumed playing. I had the same sensation again urging me to move left. Now I know what you're thinking because I was thinking that too, this is crazy, but with unquestioning faith, I cashed out my voucher and moved one machine to the left and reinserted my ticket. This continued happening until I had moved five machines to the left and arrived back beside the machine I first started at. I was now up about four hundred dollars from the original fifty dollars I had started with. It was getting late and I was about to call it a night when I looked up at the machine and saw that the jackpot had surpassed twenty-two thousand dollars. I stared at that spot on the machine and said to myself "okay, I'm going to take that home with me." It wasn't but a few moments later when the slot machine I was playing lit up. Bells started ringing and the word Jackpot started flashing across the screen. At first I could not believe it and quickly reviewed the screen in front of me. It happened! I had just won over twenty-two thousand dollars!! I tossed and turned all night I was so excited. I could not wait to get home in the morning and tell Jim. They give you this big paper sign with your name and the amount of money you've won written on it so showing that to Jim is how I told him. At first glance I guess he read it wrong because he said: "Wow, twenty-two hundred dollars, that's great, congratulations!" Then I said: "Look at it again." His face lit up in surprise and he asked "Twenty-two *thousand* dollars, seriously?" I laughed, and then took the twenty-two thousand dollars in cash I was hiding behind me and put it in his hands. We were now easily able to take care of Jordan's surgery bill. What a wonderful blessing.

As time passed Jordan's chest surgery healed incredibly well, and the scars were really only noticeable if you knew what to look for. Jordan grew more hair on his chest and began to exercise more. He was very confident to be seen without his shirt on and so he should have been! His chest looked great!

The testosterone started giving Jordan's torso a different shape, his shoulders became wider and fuller and his arms became more and more defined. Liking his new look Jordan exercised fairly regularly doing push-ups, chin-ups, sit-ups and lifting some small weights at home. He took pride in how he dressed and even smelled; yes, smelled. He became a very sharp dresser never forgetting his great smelling deodorant and cologne. All this caught the attention of the girls in school and I don't think Jordan minded one bit.

This new fancy wardrobe of Jordan's didn't come cheap, but he paid for all his clothes through the babysitting money he earned taking care of Trevor. Yes, Trevor was still around. Jordan put him on his school bus every morning and had him after school two days each week. He would also still do the occasional evening when Ashley and her husband needed a sitter. Jordan took his responsibility with Trevor very seriously and the two boys had, and still have, a wonderful bond.

One night after babysitting Trevor, Jordan told me a cute story about what had happened that evening. They had ordered a pizza and were about to watch a movie. Apparently, Trevor filled his plate with pizza and while strolling over to grab a seat on the sofa proclaimed aloud "This is the best night ever; pizza and a movie with my best friend!" That made Jordan's day.

Part of Jordan's transition was making himself as comfortable as possible with his own body. Clothing can help. Back early on, before Jordan had started his hormone replacement therapy, after one of his therapy sessions his therapist called me in. Jordan wanted her to tell me that he wanted me to buy him new underwear. He didn't know exactly how to approach the topic with me so his therapist delivered the information for him. That afternoon on the way home we stopped at Wal-Mart to shop for new underwear in the men's department. The new underwear helped but there is one very obvious piece of the male anatomy that a transgender male simply doesn't have and for them it does not go unnoticed. Soon the subject of getting Jordan a packer came up. A silicone packer is used to fill out the crotch area of clothing so it appears there is a penis. This is certainly more sophisticated than stuffing a pair of socks in your pants and can provide a more natural looking bulge. While these conversations were awkward, and a conversation I'm sure Jordan didn't enjoy having with me, we were able to discuss it and come up with some solutions. There are different types of packers, some allow for standing to pee while others do not. What might work for one person, may not work for another. The resources I provide at the back of this book are a great starting point, but you should definitely do some research of your own.

With Jordan's chest surgery behind him and his HRT (hormone replacement therapy) well established, he was in a much better place with regards to his gender dysphoria. Nevertheless, there were still more steps he desired to take before he would consider his transition complete.

CHAPTER 14

A Second Surgery

The summer between Jordan's grade nine and grade ten year was when we seriously addressed the idea of a second surgery. The possibility of this second surgery, a hysterectomy, had been on Jordan's radar for some time. Giving consideration to the magnitude of the decision the doctors preferred to wait at least a year from Jordan's previous surgery.

His age was a huge part of the consideration and, to the best of our knowledge; the surgery had not been previously done on someone as young as Jordan. This was a decision that we could not take lightly as it was a non-reversible procedure that would have life altering results.

Jordan was certain that even if he decided to have children one day it would be as a father. Even if he had the physical ability to become pregnant and carry a baby to term, he believed that to be unnatural and an emotionally impossible consideration.

Jordan expressed his thoughts and feelings to his doctors about how important this surgery was to him. They carefully evaluated his mental state as well as his physical readiness for the surgery and decided they were prepared to move forward with the procedure. With his doctors on board my husband and I consented for Jordan to have a Laser Laparoscopic Bilateral Salpingo-Oophorectomy (a surgery to remove both ovaries and both fallopian tubes also known as BSO) and a vaginal hysterectomy which is the surgical removal of the uterus through the vagina. The surgeon herself was an experienced surgeon who specializes in Obstetrics and Gynaecology and was referred to us from Jordan's endocrinologist. She had done this same surgery many times and my husband and I felt that Jordan would be in good hands.

At the time Mariah was living about four hours away from home working on an internship. She had told me previously that while she wanted to know what was going on with Jordan she did not want all the details. I wasn't sure what to do with the information. Do I tell her about Jordan's second surgery or not? I decided to call her to let her know we were going out of town with Jordan and would be staying away at least one night. I said it was for medical reasons. I left it open for her to ask me more about that but she didn't press or even ask me any questions. I concluded, perhaps wrongly so, that she wouldn't want to know. In addition to Jim and me, the only people that knew the surgery was taking place were my parents, my cousin Leanne, and a close family friend named, Julianna. Julianna and I had been friends since our eldest children were in kindergarten and just like with Leanne, there is little that goes on in my life that I don't share with her.

It was almost exactly one year after Jordan's chest surgery when he found himself on the operating table once more. This second surgery was performed in an operating room at a large hospital in South Western Ontario. Unlike Jordan's chest surgery, this surgery was covered by our province's health care plan. Post surgery, Jordan would also be able to stop taking his twice daily nasal spray (Suprefact Nasal). I was glad for that because we still did not know what the long term side effects of the drug were, if any.

On the day of the surgery my friend Julianna drove a few hours from her home to offer support to Jim and I. I was grateful for the extra company and the distraction having her there brought us. Even though this was Jordan's second surgery, I was no more at ease than first time he went under the knife. It wasn't any less stressful and the waiting was still the worst part. The actual surgery took about three hours but it was closer to four before we were able to see Jordan. Julianna stayed until Jim and I were with him and she was able to see for herself that Jordan was okay.

Jordan was set up in a private room and we were given an update from his surgical team who assured us everything went very well. Jordan was in a lot of pain when he awoke and was feeling anxious about having to leave the hospital that same day. It seems crazy but they really were looking to discharge him just hours after his surgery. Arrangements had been made for the three of us to stay at Ronald McDonald house that evening so we did not have to make the two hour drive home. Jim, Julianna and I went over there to take a look around and get checked in while Jordan was still in surgery. Jim got our overnight bags in from the car and placed them in our room. Having all this done before hand simplified things for later when Jordan was discharged. We were able to move Jordan between the hospital and Ronald McDonald house in a wheelchair that the hospital loaned us for the night.

Ronald McDonald house is an amazing place. There was everything you could need including a full kitchen, dining, gaming and relaxing areas throughout the main floor. The scale of each room was large enough to accommodate many visitors and all the common areas were bright and cheerfully decorated. An elevator took us to our second storey room which was great because Jordan was in no condition to walk up stairs. The generous size of the room and bathroom made it easy manoeuvring Jordan's wheelchair around. One of the first things we noticed upon entering the room was a beautiful blue and cream coloured blanket at the end of one of the two beds. It was tied up with a thick cream coloured satin ribbon and had a personal note attached. While I can't recall exactly what the note said, it was addressed to Jordan and stated that the homemade blanket was a gift for him that he could take home as a reminder of his time at Ronald McDonald house. What a wonderful and thoughtful gift. After we got Jordan comfortably into bed I was able to slip away for a few minutes to give my parents a quick call. Just outside the room, at the end of the corridor there was a quiet seating area with a comfy couch, chair and large wooden desk. On the desk there was a courtesy phone guests could use which I happily availed myself of. I phoned my parents to give them an update. I had already sent a text to them and to Leanne from the hospital letting them know Jordan had come through surgery and that everything went well. The phone call was more to fill them in on some of the details and to let them know that Jordan was all settled in for the night. I told them if everything went as expected we would be heading home in the morning. Honestly, it was a blessing to know we were just across the parking lot to the hospital in case any complications arose that first night. Other than the expected post surgery pain and discomfort, there were no complications.

Even though we only needed to stay one night, many families rely on Ronald McDonald house to be their home away from home for much longer. It is a resource for families with children either in hospital or just out of hospital who do not reside in the area. You can find them near major medical facilities in many major cities. We are very appreciative for Ronald McDonald House and what they did for us in the short time we were there.

The pain after the surgery was very real and the next morning Jordan was dreading the drive home. He was extremely uncomfortable during the drive but handled it with so much more grace than I think I could have mustered. Jordan was given some strong pain medication to manage the pain for the first seven days. As it turned out he was able to wean himself off of it after only a few days. By the end of the third day, he was able to manage the discomfort with Advil. Even though there was a lot of pain, perhaps much more than he expected, his relief following the surgery was evident. His recovery was swift and he returned to school in a little over a week. He still had to be careful not to lift anything heavy or strain himself in order to avoid complications, of which he had none. I marvelled at how resilient his body was and how quickly he was able to bounce back.

CHAPTER 15

New Identification: Challenging the Bureaucracy

The reason we put off changing Jordan's gender marker on his ID before this point was because of the way our provincial health care plan was set up. By waiting until after Jordan's second surgery, his second surgery was covered by OHIP. Had we changed his gender marker (at least on his health card) to male prior to his BSO and Hysterectomy, the cost of that surgery would not have been covered. Fortunately, we were alerted to this fact so we knew about it and could plan accordingly.

Getting new identification like a new birth certificate, new social insurance number, passport, driver's licence, and health card is not an easy task for a minor. One might think that if there is a parent to advocate for the child, it would be straightforward. We quickly found it was not.

I will share with you the details of the struggle we went through to get Jordan his new identification and the steps we took to overcome some of the bureaucratic roadblocks. Even if you do not live in Ontario or even in Canada for that matter, there are still some valuable lessons in this chapter. If you want to see a change in your own jurisdiction, I encourage you to fight for that change just like Jordan and I did. One person can make a difference and in our case it was not only about helping Jordan but helping to pave the way for those that come after him.

We started the process after Jordan's second surgery. This was roughly four months before his sixteenth birthday. I expected that by planning that far ahead, we would be able to have Jordan's new identification in hand by the time his birthday rolled around. This was not to be. We came up against seemingly endless government roadblocks. I expect that regardless of the Province or State many transgender children and teens live in, they experience these same issues.

A year earlier, I had looked into the law regarding changing the gender marker on a birth certificate. I learned, that at the time, a person must have undergone at least one sex reassignment surgery and present a medical letter along with their application in order to qualify for a gender marker change in Ontario. Jordan had already undergone two surgeries and had been on testosterone for almost two full years. We also had multiple letters signed from his doctors saying the gender change was not only appropriate but was in Jordan's best interest. Therefore, he more than met the requirements for a new birth certificate to be issued with a male gender marker.

First, I downloaded all the appropriate name change and gender change forms from our provincial government's website. I thought it made sense to send in both the name change and gender change applications at the same time so only one new birth certificate would need to be printed. Makes perfect sense, right? Anyway, the name change form was very straightforward. It had to be signed by both my husband and myself (the legal guardians of the child) and signed by someone like a doctor or minister, someone who could claim they knew Jordan had lived in the province for at least two years. There was also another form we could include if we wished to keep this name change from appearing in the newspaper, which we did. Normally, all name changes are publicly released; however, they make an exception in Ontario when the name change is being done for a transgender person.

The gender change application was far more detailed and did require at least one doctor's letter advocating for the gender change. It wasn't until I came across a page that spoke in first person and was to be witnessed by a notary republic that "I" being a person over eighteen years was changing my gender. As soon as I saw that, I stopped filling out the form and called the office of the government where the form was to be submitted. I asked them how they wanted me to fill out the page. I asked if I should just cross out all the "I's" and replace with "We" and have my husband and I both sign because I was the one actually submitting the application; or did they want Jordan to fill it. If he filled it out, I suggested my husband and I could also sign as the persons over eighteen. They advised me to do neither, saying that if I altered the form in any way, it would be rejected. They also informed me that there was no way to submit an application for gender change for a person less than eighteen years of age. I was outraged. How could this be? Age was not part of the requirements when I called the year before. Jordan had already met all the necessary requirements they gave me at the time. There absolutely had to be a way around this and so I immediately began to try to find one.

I reached out to Egale, Canada's Human Rights Trust. The purpose of this organization is to help in the advancement of equality, diversity, education and justice for the LGBTQ community. Through speaking with Egale I learned that the rules around when someone could change their gender marker had changed since my inquiry a year earlier. I didn't even know there was a law change in the works. A representative from Egale told me they had been one of the organizations the government consulted when considering making a change to the existing law. In fact, Egale offered quite a bit of feedback on the matter. Egale had been trying to get the law changed for some time on behalf of transgender people. Prior to April of 2013 the law was that surgery was required and Egale was arguing that it was unjust to force a transgender person to go under the knife in order to change their gender marker to one that matched their gender identity. Many transgender people are happy and content to achieve their outward appearance by binding, hairstyles and clothing alone. That law was discrimination, plain and simple.

The problem was that when the government agreed to change the law and remove the surgical requirement they had inserted, without consultation from Egale, an age restriction of eighteen years, which had previously not been part of the law. Now, as it was, Jordan was caught between two laws. Under the old law he qualified for the gender marker change but under this new law he did not.

I thought there must be some way around this so I reached out to local heads of government both in writing and by phone. As hard as I tried to get someone to give me a straight answer I just kept getting pushed around from one person or department to another. In the end, I landed back with the manager at Service Ontario. I asked the Service Ontario Manager how I could get around the current form and file the application for gender change so it would be accepted. Again, I was told that because Jordan was a minor, and the current law states you must be eighteen years old to change the gender on a birth certificate, there was no way she could assist me.

After speaking on the phone, I forwarded this manager documentation of my son's situation. This included doctors' letters and a large picture collage I had prepared showing photos of

Jordan going all the way back to age three. The photos all depicted a male gender expression which I hoped would support our case. There were pictures taken at home, on vacations, karate class, and his grade eight graduation. The common thread among them all being his consistent male gender expression. Honestly, no one could look at the collage and conclude the child in the photos was a girl. I wanted the pictures to help them reach the same conclusion which we had reached. It would be ludicrous to expect Jordan to continue on with a female gender marker. It worked, or at least it got some attention. The Service Ontario manager called me back to say she would put forth a proposal to see if they could get this issue put on the calendar. She would try to see if there was a way to have the current law reviewed again.

The lawmakers actually called a meeting to vote on whether or not they could have a meeting on reviewing the law. How crazy does that sound? They needed to hold a meeting in order to decide whether or not the subject warranted another meeting. If they concluded it did warrant another meeting it would be put on the schedule. Getting a meeting put on the schedule would mean they had agreed to at least discuss the current law and hopefully they would consider making changes. I was warned this could take months, possibly even a year or more before we could see any movement on this. If it did take that long, Jordan could already be eighteen by the time they reached a conclusion. I felt strongly it was well worth fighting for. Even if it did not happen before Jordan turned eighteen, if we got them to change the law it could help those younger than him in the same situation, so we pushed on.

Jordan asked me if he could write a letter to the government advocating for himself. I thought that was a terrific idea. I told Jordan if he wrote it, I would see it got to the appropriate person. I would like to share his letter with you,

To Whom It May Concern,

I am Jordan James Evans. That's the name I feel fits anyways. My legal name is Jordan Catherine Evans. I am a male student attending secondary school in Southern Ontario. At least that's a sentence that I feel describes myself. Legally though, female would be more accurate.

The term transgender does not resonate with me how you might think it should. I don't place myself in that category. I am just a teenage boy, not a trans-guy, not an FTM, not a transgender male. Just a teenage boy, that's who I am. I don't generally think about being transgender or the topic of transgender because I don't like to, it reminds me that in some sense, I do fall under that category.

When I had my hysterectomy, I was not thinking about it as though I was having SRS (sex reassignment surgery). I was just thinking of it as another surgery. Bottom line, transgender isn't on my mind, but it does exist.

My gender marker on any legal document of mine has a big fat "F" on it, for female. That F shouldn't be there. However, it is. It will be there every single time I cross the border. It will be there when I apply for my first job, and it will be there when I go to get my drivers licence.

All my friends are getting jobs. One of my friends even offered me a job; he said he could put in a good word for me and get me an interview right around Christmas time if I wanted. I told him no, that I was good but thanks for the offer. Our economy in southern Ontario isn't the best since the auto industry crashed everyone knows that. Do you know how rare it is to have a decent job opportunity handed to you like that? I said no. I'm scared to apply, scared to go through gender confusion issues. I am not confused, but can you imagine what they'd think, looking at me, compared to my paper/identification?

Having that "F" on all my legal documents confuses a lot of situations that shouldn't be confusing at all. I need you to change it! The fact that the law says only someone over eighteen has the right to be viewed as who they are isn't okay. What about me? I've already had two SRS surgeries, so why won't you let me change my "F" to an "M"? I need this to be done, and I need it done NOW. Just because I am not eighteen does not mean I don't feel the effects of having the wrong gender marker on my legal papers.

If, at the very least, you won't let me make the change, you should definitely let my parents make the change on my behalf. If I were a baby born intersexed, you would let my parents decide my gender for me and proceed to put that on my birth record, so they should be able to act as legal guardian now in the same way.

Sincerely,
Jordan Evans

Jordan brought up many good points in his letter, but in the end it didn't matter. We still had to wait for them to have their meetings and decide whether or not they would review the law. This left us no other choice than to wait. Frustrated, I contacted Egale again and they referred me to a lawyer in Toronto. This lawyer was interested in assisting Jordan with his fight for gender change and offered to look into the case for us pro-bono. In the meantime she strongly suggested we go ahead and submit Jordan's name change request. Jordan was looking to change only his middle name from a female name to a male name, one he had chosen for himself. Our lawyer advised us that once we got the name change done there was a possibility we could use that along with a doctor's letter to change Jordan's Social Insurance Card and possibly even to apply for a driver's licence and passport with a male gender marker. I went ahead and filed the paperwork. Jordan's sixteenth birthday was now only one month away.

While we waited for Jordan's name change papers to come through, his sixteenth birthday came and went. Then finally a few weeks later, his new birth certificate arrived showing his new name. Of course, the gender was still F for female but it was a first step.

With the new birth certificate in hand we went to our local Service Ontario office to apply for a new provincial health card and social insurance card. We needed to show Jordan's certificate of name change along with the new birth certificate and one doctor's letter stating that Jordan should have his id changed to male.

Surprisingly, this process was quite easy and within just a few weeks Jordan's new SIN (social insurance number) card and new health card arrived in the mail. While we were at the Service Ontario office I happened to notice that you could apply for a provincial photo ID card if you did not have a driver's licence. The cost for this card was thirty-five dollars. Jordan would need to have photo ID, his birth certificate, name change certificate and a doctor's letter to apply.

I looked into him getting his driver's licence and found that a provincial photo ID card is all that Jordan would need to apply for a license. If we could get that card for him with an "M" on it, it would remove a lot of awkwardness at the Ministry of Transportation. Until we realized this was acceptable ID, the only choice we had was to use the birth certificate and they would license him with a female marker. If we got the photo ID card first, he could apply for his license with that and have his license issued with a male gender marker. We were told by Service Ontario that, in order to obtain this photo ID card Jordan would need to provide something with his photo and signature on it. His new health card would work perfectly once it arrived in the mail. It would have his male gender marker in addition to both his signature and photo on it. In case we didn't want to wait for that to arrive, because it could take a couple weeks or more by mail, we were offered a second option. We were told we could return the next day with Jordan's Canadian passport which would have a photo and signature. They said they would accept his passport even though the gender marker hadn't been changed yet. We opted to do the latter for the sole reason it would get us the photo ID card faster.

The next day we went back with Jordan's passport and all the other ID we had previously provided for the new Health Card and after paying the $35 fee they completed all the paperwork for Jordan's new photo ID card. The great news is it would come with his correct male gender marker! The new photo ID card was the first of the three new pieces of ID to arrive in the mail. Jordan was so happy to finally have something he could use that truly represented who he was.

Jordan immediately prepared for his written driver's test. As soon as he felt ready we went to the Ministry of Transportation Vehicle Testing Center. He presented his new Ontario Photo ID card without issue. Then wrote and passed his G1 drivers test. Even though he only had the photo ID card for a very short time it allowed him to walk into the driver's training centre and apply for his licence without anyone knowing anything about his past. Once he passed his test he had to relinquish the photo ID card which they replaced with his new driver's license. In Ontario, you can't hold both an Ontario photo ID card and a driver's licence at the same time. It was still worth getting; because it saved Jordan a lot of grief and was the only piece of ID he needed to show to write the driver's test. His driver's licence was issued with the correct gender marker, male. Jordan was very happy.

Within just a few short weeks his new health card and social insurance card also came in the mail. With a new SIN card and driver's license, Jordan was free to go apply for a job as the male that he is. Our only other obstacles at this point were the passport and the birth certificate (remember the newly issued birth certificate only changed his name, not his gender). It was looking more and more like the birth certificate issue would not be resolved until after his eighteenth birthday. Putting that aside for now, we turned to the passport.

Passports are a document issued by the Federal Government, not the Provincial Government, and I had been told it would not be easy. The passport isn't a big issue for a lot of teenagers but we do travel to the U.S. on a regular basis and each time it involved a lot of explaining including showing a doctor's note. This was because Jordan did not look female which was the gender listed on his passport. The photo was older, taken just before Jordan cut his hair and began taking testosterone. So, not only was the gender marker incorrect, he didn't look anything like the person in the picture. Something we discussed was that if the Federal Government will not allow us to change the gender marker on the passport before Jordan turned eighteen; we could always re-apply with a new photo. At least that way, the photo on the passport would look like Jordan, but honestly, this was not an acceptable solution for us and we were not prepared to settle with just an updated photo.

I phoned the Canadian Passport office and explained that our Province had already changed Jordan's Health Card, Social Insurance Card and issued a Provincial Photo ID Card all showing the appropriate gender. I waited silently on the phone for what I expected would be another hurdle or battle we would have to overcome. To my surprise there were no more hurdles to jump or battles to fight. Their reply was that it could be done. All we needed to do to have his gender changed on his passport was to fill out a new passport application and submit a doctor's letter, which we already had. Jordan had new passport photos taken right away and we took the passport application and doctor's letter (as requested) into our local passport office. There were no problems! Jordan received his new passport within a few weeks by mail and it was complete with his new name, gender and photo. Not only did it arrive sooner than expected, but it is valid for ten years.

Just before preparing this book for publication, I read about Australia taking a huge step forward in the fight for gender equality. It appears they are the first country to remove gender from their passports and driver's licences. This will help so many transgender Australians avoid the uncomfortable issues that they may currently face because their gender expression does not match the gender marker on their identification papers. Kudos to Australia!

For now, Jordan's ID issues are all sorted out, with the exception of his birth certificate of course. Honestly, that just doesn't seem to be as important anymore. He can travel with his new passport, get a job with his new social insurance card, and even go to the doctor or a walk in clinic with his new health card and was already driving with his new driver's licence. He will want to have the birth certificate changed when he is eighteen but until then all the usual identification a person uses on a regular basis had been updated. This made for one very happy young man.

The lawyer we had been working with told me that I could fight for his birth certificate to be changed in court, before he turned eighteen. She said that we could try to get a judge to allow Jim and me to change the gender marker on Jordan's birth certificate as his legal guardians. Fighting for our parental rights could take one to two years to play out in the courts. This would mean Jordan's eighteenth birthday could arrive before a legal solution could be reached. We opted not to go the legal route and instead continued trying to fight for a law change at the provincial level. It was, after all, the law that needed to be changed for everyone's sake. Getting a judgment for Jordan wasn't going to serve the bigger picture. He was definitely not the only youth in this situation.

I placed another call to the Service Ontario manager to follow up and see if there had been any movement. She told me a meeting had been held and the outcome was positive. It was agreed they would revisit the law regarding changing gender on a birth certificate as it relates to minors. It had been put on the schedule. Apparently, they had put forth a motion to bring this law back before the government to review and discuss the possibility of rewriting it, or at the very least adding a provision to accommodate for minors. These things do not happen overnight and we still didn't know if anything would be done before Jordan turned eighteen, but at least they had agreed to revisit it. It is progress in the right direction.

Fast forward about seven months, I received a call from the Service Ontario Manager I had been speaking with earlier about getting transgender minors birth certificates changed. During this call, I was told that our efforts had gotten some attention and they were now working on changing the rules for minors and that they would update us again once they knew more. About two or three months later I got another call from the same Service Ontario manager asking me if Jordan and I would be willing to complete a survey. They advised us that we could complete the survey anonymously. The questions were centered around our feelings on the current law and how we felt it should be changed. We were told that our answers would be helpful to the government in revisiting this legislation. They wanted each of us to complete it so they could see the responses from both the parent's view as well as the child's. Jordan and I were happy to comply with anything that would get us closer to changing the law in Ontario. Later that same day, the surveys were sent to me by email. There was one marked for the child and one for the parent but they were essentially the same survey. Jordan and I began working on them right away.

I was impressed by Jordan's responses on the survey as they were very well thought out and more reasonable than I expected. I guess I thought they would be all pro-change without a lot of consideration for different circumstances. Jordan told me that he recognized that there is a vast difference in the level of maturity amongst his peers and as such saw a need to be conscientious with regards to what protocols should be in place before a minor can change their gender.

The questions on the survey focused mainly on our opinions as to what the rules and requirements should be around a minor being allowed to change their gender. The survey contained three pages of questions. Here are just a few to give you an idea of what was being asked: "At what age do you feel it should be allowed that gender can be changed on a birth certificate?" "Should surgery be required?" "Should parental consent; be required and if so by both parents?" "In the case of divorce where one parent has sole custody should the non custodial parent have to be notified before a change can be made?" "Should change be allowed to be made without the child's consent?" "At what age can a child give consent?" We happily filled out the surveys and submitted them back within a couple of days. Then, we waited again for an update.

I owe a great thanks to the lawyer who consulted with me on this and advised me to forget the birth certificate and start with the name change and then go after the health card and social insurance cards next. I just wish that our provincial government had advised me of this. As it would have resulted in us getting all this done months earlier. I did phone the manager I had been speaking to at Service Ontario back and advised her about the success we had in changing Jordan's identification. It was my hope that her staff could offer the same suggestions our lawyer did and make the next person's battle a little easier.

To my surprise, it was only about five months later when I received another call from the Service Ontario manager. She called to advise me that they had made the decision to change the law and allow minors to apply for a change of gender on both their birth certificates and birth registrations. This was huge! She told me that at this point they were preparing the actual application for minors. Once the applications were finished and available to be sent out she would immediately send us one for Jordan. When I asked about how long before we could expect the application to be available, she said it could take up to three months. I told Jordan, first chance I got, about the latest development and said it was now possible we could get his birth records updated before he turned eighteen.

The application came through as we had been told it would about three months later. We wasted no time in filling it out and got it back into Service Ontario. I'd like to share some of that letter with you: "*I'm pleased to inform you of new criteria to allow children 17 years of age and under to change the sex designation on their Ontario birth registration. Ensuring that transgender children are offered the same opportunity as adults is part of the government's commitment to build a fair and inclusive society.*" The letter went on to say *"for added flexibility, applicants 16 or 17 years of age have the option to apply as adults or children."*

Within six weeks of submitting his application, my son received his new birth certificate showing his gender as male. It felt as if the road before us was so long and the task so daunting when it all started but now, looking back, even over all the twists and turns, it was a fight worth fighting. I believe it was only through persistence and determination that this law got changed. I think many people push against government and when government pushes back or makes it challenging, people simply give up or lose their desire to fight for change, no matter how badly they want it. Even though Jordan's desire is to maintain privacy about his identity, it is rewarding for him to know that his actions (with a little help from his mom), have made a difference in Ontario.

We continue to make advancements in the fight for the rights of transgender people. In May of 2016 Canada's Prime Minister

Justin Trudeau announced he was putting forth a new legislative bill. The bill will extend human rights protections to all transgender people in Canada. This new legislation, if passed, would make it illegal to discriminate based on gender identity and gender expression. Ontario was one of the Canadian provinces with similar legislation already in place, but now Justin Trudeau was setting a bill into action that could ensure these rights across all of Canada.

Change does come even though it may not arrive as swiftly as we would like it to. The important thing is that we continue to rally for what we believe is important and push and challenge our governments, regardless of where we are geographically in the world. Things only improve when enough people stand up and fight. Don't give up. Keep pushing, keep fighting, you may be only one person but your voice does matter.

CHAPTER 16

Which Washroom?

Not to open a can of worms here, but this topic is racing like a freight train out of control and there are some things that I feel need to be said. News of public officials attempting to legislate which washrooms transgender people should use seems to be popping up everywhere, especially on the World Wide Web. I can't even go on facebook these days without my news feed filling up with unwelcomed, often down right hateful comments about transgender people and the washroom debate. My personal opinion is that the people trying to force others to use the washroom that matches their birth sex rather than their gender identity do not fully understand what it is to be transgender.

The most basic thing about transgender people is they truly believe they are the gender they identify with! Transgender women do not think of themselves as men wearing women's clothing, they ARE women. Naturally, they should be in a woman's washroom. They need the facilities just like everyone else. Transgender women, while seen by many as only biological men, don't share this same thought process. They do not identify as men at all. Asking them to use the men's washroom is like asking a non-trans woman to use the men's washroom. It just does not make any sense.

Two months into the year of 2016, the number of bills targeting the rights of transgender people in the United States was more than double the total amount of bills for all of 2015. This is according to a report put out by the Human Rights Campaign (HRC). This report can be found on their website: www.hrc.org. Many of these bills are aimed at transgender children and about half of them appear to be related to student washrooms. In my opinion, these bills are not reducing discrimination or making advances in the fight against discrimination but only serve to set us back years with respect to LGBT rights.

On television, commercials are being aired showing men following little girls into washrooms sending a fear based message to the public. It seems irrational to me that a fear of sexual assault can somehow justify keeping transgender persons out of the washrooms with which they identify.

Now, arguably, it may be cross-dressers that these washroom naysayers are concerned about rather than with transgender people. I would expect most cross-dressers have, at one time or another, been on the receiving end of some very nasty discrimination, hate or even bullying. This, in my opinion, makes them highly unlikely to be aggressors themselves. What is important to note is that cross-dressers are not transgender people. Cross-dressers don't share the same disconnect between their biological sex and their brains interpretation of their gender. I do confess there is an argument here. It is a difficult thing to police because visibly I do not know how one can distinguish between a cross-dresser and a transgender person without asking them straight out how they identify.

It is difficult for me to envision that a pedophile or rapist would slip into a dress just to weasel their way into a woman's washroom. I am also unaware of any statistics that support this theory. Keeping transgender people out of the washrooms they identify with is certainly not the answer.

Some pedophiles prey on young boys. However, there are no laws popping up that say grown men can not use the same washroom as little boys. There are already laws in place that say it is illegal to assault another person. So, let's be honest. These types of washroom laws have little to do with protecting innocent people, namely women and young girls. They are about discriminating against, hating and even fearing a group of individuals that are so grossly misunderstood by so many members of society.

If fear is not the motivation for proposing such discriminatory laws, then the only other motivation I can see is one based on religion. Some right-wing extremists or religious conservatives may feel that a transgender person offends their religious belief that "God makes no mistakes," there is only male and female. They may want to use the legal system to punish or force compliance with their religious beliefs. I am far from a right wing extremist but I actually do believe the statement, "God makes no mistakes." My belief about gender goes beyond just male and female. I believe in a gender definition that places us not just on the outer ends of a gender spectrum where male and female reside, but anywhere along that spectrum. I believe God was purposeful in putting transgender people on this earth. They certainly have a rather unique perspective on the world. They can also teach us a few things about compassion, understanding, tolerance and diversity.

The anti-LGBT North Carolina public bathroom bill, officially titled HB2 (House Bill 2) set a new precedent. This bill singles out and specifically targets transgender people. This bill, which was passed in March of 2016, made North Carolina the first state to enact such a law. This law sets us back decades with regards to LGBT human rights. The ironic thing about this law is that it does the exact opposite of what it was expected to do when it comes to keeping men from using women's washrooms. HB2 says an individual must use the washroom that matches the gender on their birth certificate.

First thing you should know is that birth certificates, in some states and provinces (like in Ontario, Canada where I live), can be changed. In other states and provinces, birth certificates cannot be changed. This means that there are some transgender people who have changed their birth certificates and some who have not.

The rules regarding when you can change your birth certificate also vary. The reality is that a transgender person could actually, in some places, get the gender on their birth certificate changed without having any genital surgery. It is actually possible that a transgender woman could have a birth certificate that says she is female, even though she still has a penis. She would be legally using a ladies washroom in North Carolina under their new bill. So, for those who support HB2, know, that in the example I just used, HB2 does not serve to keep male anatomy out of the ladies room. The only transgender women HB2 is keeping from the ladies room are those that have not been able to change their birth certificates.

Now consider a transgender man who has been on hormone therapy for some time. He presents as fully male on the exterior, so you are unable to tell that he is actually a transgender man by looking at him. Anyone would naturally assume he is a non-transgender man. If, for whatever reason, this transgender man has not changed his birth certificate from female, under the HB2 law, he will be required to use the ladies room. Any woman in the washroom at the time he enters would absolutely presume he was a man. The reality is he IS a man, a transgender man. Just because he has not changed his birth certificate doesn't mean he is not a man. I understand that while some religious folks may disagree with me on this, their disagreement is not relevant to understand what I am telling you. What I want you to understand is that this transgender man, under the North Carolina HB2 law, will be required to use the ladies room.

Like many of the anti-LGBT proposals on the books, HB2 seems to overlook the "Law of Unintended Consequences." The law of unintended consequences, simply put, means that actions *always* include results that are unanticipated. Using HB2 as an example it appears that even the most basic consequences have not been anticipated.

North Carolina lawmakers had the intent that HB2 would keep biological men from entering a ladies room. Before this law, there were transgender women (born biological men) using the ladies room. Transgender people have existed for decades. Where do you think they have been until now? They have been using the washrooms they identify with.

This bill recognizes transgender men only as biological women and regardless of how masculine their outward appearance is HB2 dictates that transgender men belong in the ladies room. A transgender woman, even one whose outward appearance does not completely conceal their masculine history in the ladies room would not alarm me. I would see her for who she is, a transgender woman.

With this law in place, it makes it much easier, not harder, for non-transgender men to enter the ladies room. Now, any man looking to do harm doesn't even need to dress the part of a woman to gain access to the ladies room. With HB2 in place, he can just enter and claim to be a transgender man. Of course, this would be illegal, but with the law requiring transgender men to use the ladies room, he can just blend in.

One thing is for certain; if my son Jordan ever entered a woman's washroom, alarm bells would ring! Jordan presents completely male. If, as a transgender man, he is not allowed to use the men's washroom, I guarantee you it would cause much more upset with him in the ladies room. Also, how would anyone in the men's washroom know he was transgender in the first place? They wouldn't unless there are hidden cameras in the washroom stalls. Now, that would definitely be a cause for concern.

Transgender men and women will be at risk of humiliation, embarrassment and possible bullying. This could happen because this law forces them to use a washroom that in most cases is completely opposite of their gender expression and certainly opposite to their gender identity.

This law does nothing to protect anyone, but certainly has tremendous power to do a whole lot of harm. Ironically, this whole thing seems so unnecessary. Things were fine the way they were. Transgender people had been quietly going about their business, no pun intended, in the washroom they were most comfortable using for years. The motto: "If it isn't broken, don't fix it" seems to fit here.

HB2 has garnered a lot of attention and has also prompted

some large companies to react. Fortunately, the companies I have been reading about take a stand against states that discriminate. Some of them cancelling or putting on hold expansion plans in North Carolina, while others going so far as to move their businesses out of the discriminating state altogether. Companies that have already taken a stand include: PayPal, Google Ventures, Lionsgate Films, and Deutsche Bank. I applaud these companies for their bold and decisive moves.

Well known entertainers including Bruce Springsteen, Ringo Star, Nick Jonas and Demi Lovato have cancelled performances scheduled in North Carolina as a way to use their voices to stand up for human rights and show their distaste for bill HB2. Others like Cyndi Lauper and Mumford & Son's decided to push forward with their concerts saying they will be donating all the proceeds to an LGBT charity. Many other high profile people are also speaking out and their voices are not going unheard. Just a couple months after this law came out, the state of North Carolina had reportedly already lost hundreds of millions of dollars in business and yet lawmakers appear to be digging their heels in even more. A hotline was set up so people could report anyone presumed to be breaking the law. Is it any wonder why transgender folks fear using public washrooms? Like I mentioned in an earlier chapter, even my son Jordan struggled with this early in his transition and a negative health issue resulted because of it.

It is not justifiable to discriminate against a group of individuals whose gender identity does not line up neatly with society's traditional binary definitions of gender. Society has, by tradition, dictated the custom that women use women's washrooms and men use men's washrooms. However, to the best of my knowledge before HB2 became law in North Carolina, there were no laws in North America that states it was against the law to ignore these customs. This notion of legislating washroom use seems to be a solution in search of a problem. Washroom use is dictated by societal norms. Why should we attempt to make washroom use a legal matter?

I have seen people in dire need of a toilet rush into the opposite washroom when the line to theirs was too long. Parents often accompany small children into washrooms, putting either the child or the parent in the 'wrong' washroom. Family washrooms appear to be society's response to these situations. However, family washrooms are not always available. Are we going to make these situations illegal; or are we going to blatantly attempt to legally discriminate against a specific group, namely anyone who is transgender? I suppose North Carolina has already decided on what it wants to do.

In the spring of 2016, in the state of Kansas, a bill was created that would financially reward students for reporting transgender students in school washrooms. This bill is formally called "The Student Physical Privacy Act." If it passes and becomes law it would give students the right to sue the school, and collect up to twenty-five hundred dollars, if they report a transgender person using the 'wrong' washroom. This bill claims it will help protect students from having to share their washroom with a transgender person. This, in my mind, is a very dangerous bill that encourages bullying.

By providing a monetary reward or bounty to students for outing transgender persons, policy makers could actually be grossly diminishing privacy for everyone. Students could become so motivated by the cash bounty that they invade the privacy of all students in an effort to uncover their transgender school mates. Students often have limited financial resources which, for some, could make this twenty-five hundred dollar motivation hard to resist. What lengths do you think students will go to in order to make themselves twenty-five hundred dollars richer? I for one do not like to even think about it. When I do, I picture cameras in washrooms and everyone's privacy being invaded, all in an effort to expose a vulnerable few. This is just another example, in my opinion of course; of misguided lawmakers creating situations that have the potential to cause great harm. This bill, if made law, could inadvertently cause situations which yield results far outside their intended scope. Results could include increasing the already horrifically high suicide rates among our youth, transgender or not. Thankfully, the reality is that this particular bill was introduced too late for it to even be read during the current legislative session. While put forth as proposed legislation, in all likelihood it was probably more of a 'trial balloon' to gauge public support in the state of Kansas for such legislation moving forward.

In an earlier chapter, I talked about the arrangements Jordan's primary school had made for him to use the staff washrooms in order to make everyone feel more comfortable. While this isn't always the best answer, at the time, it was for Jordan. This was because he wasn't yet comfortable walking into the boy's washroom and, once out as a transgender male, the girls washroom did not seem to fit either. It is difficult when on a Thursday you are in school with a female gender expression and the following Monday your gender expression is male. It was far more comfortable for Jordan to make the washroom transition when the following school year began, at his new school - which is exactly what he did. Undeniably, I was still learning about transgenderism back then and honestly didn't recognize that using a gender neutral washroom could send a harmful message. Each person is going to handle the early stages of their transition differently. Some are going to want to have everything switch on a dime others may want more time to ease into things. There is no right or wrong answer. It all boils down to the individual's gender dysphoria and what makes the most sense for them at the time. Hopefully, what they want and what the school wants are the same but there is no guarantee that will be the case.

Thankfully, these laws no longer impact Jordan because he is fortunate enough to live in a place where he was able to get his birth certificate changed. While we do not live in North Carolina or any of the other states currently entertaining such discriminatory laws, we do travel to some of them. Some transgender people may live in a place that doesn't allow for birth certificates to be changed or they may not yet qualify. Some may choose to leave their birth certificate unchanged as a matter of personal choice. It is those that have a birth certificate that differs from their gender identity who will suffer the most under these laws.

I do suspect that individuals who have a strong gender expression, one that does not raise suspicion, will choose to go against laws like HB2. Even without a birth certificate to support their gender identity my feeling is they will spare themselves the humiliation and just go ahead and use the washroom with which they identify; despite the law. Unless someone is following them into the private stall, no one will be the wiser anyway and everyone can go about their business in peace.

I tried to have this conversation with someone who is a supporter of bill HB2 and their comment to me was "they (referring to transgender people) should use the family washroom." Seriously! Should transgender people sit at the back of the bus too? I thought we had gotten past the disgraceful act of segregating people. The realization is that we really have not got past it at all. When you think of gender segregation, we have always done that by way of having separate men's and ladies' rooms. With many people living their lives outside of society's binary roles for male and female these issues need to be addressed.

Ultimately, it comes down to a human rights issue. Most people take the simplest things in life for granted, like being able to pee in a washroom they relate to. Shouldn't everyone share that right? There are passionately held views around this subject and sometimes people's tempers flare. What's disheartening is that real people are getting hurt in the crossfire, admittedly on both sides.

As you read these words, it is my personal hope that the laws I am writing about have already been repealed or were never enacted in the first place. There is something positive that has resulted from all this craziness and that is that more and more people are hearing the word transgender for the first time. As people are taking notice, some are actually taking the time and initiative to investigate the topic for themselves personally, like Pastor Mark Wingfield of Dallas. He wrote an article entitled "Seven Things I'm Learning About Transgender Persons" which was posted on baptistnews.com May 13, 2016. In his article, he shared that he had enlisted the help of a paediatrician and a geneticist in order to become more knowledgeable on the topic. The article garnered a lot of attention on social media further helping to spread awareness. I think churches would be more welcoming and inclusive places if more pastors delved into further educating themselves on the topic.

Meanwhile, as North Americans continue to argue over which washroom a transgender woman should use, halfway around the world in Tel Aviv, they celebrate the femininity of transgender women with a "Miss Trans Israel 2016" beauty pageant. Other places like Barcelona, Naples and Thailand hold similar contests each year. This demonstrates how far we still have to go with regards to understanding, acknowledging and even respecting transgender people here in North America.

We had begun to evolve from the discriminatory injustices of our past. However, laws like HB2 seem to be moving us backwards, erasing decades of progress. Some say ignorance is bliss. That may be true in some instances, but it can be downright dangerous if you are in a position to influence law making. For those transgender people that live stealth lives, forcing them, by law, to use the washroom of their birth sex could not only upset others in that washroom but also cause real problems for the transgender person. I guess the naysayers haven't fully thought this one all the way through!

CHAPTER 17

Dealt Another Blow

Just when things were starting to settle down, Jordan was dealt another blow. It happened one evening almost two years from the date Jordan began his hormone therapy. He was in the kitchen heating up some leftovers, Mariah was sitting just outside the kitchen at our dining room table, I was in the living room, and my husband was out of the house.

Mariah and I heard a utensil drop on the kitchen floor and thought nothing of it. Jordan must have dropped a spoon, no big deal. Then I hear Mariah ask Jordan: "What the heck are you doing?" Seconds later, I heard a loud thud and ran into the kitchen to see Jordan having a seizure on the kitchen floor.

Apparently, Mariah saw him seizing while he was still standing at the counter but thought he was just acting weird. It wasn't until he began to fall back she realized something was seriously wrong.

Mariah got on the phone right away and called 911 while I attended to Jordan. I had seen other people have seizures before so I immediately recognized that this was what was happening. The seizure itself lasted for less than five minutes, but it felt like forever! Mariah was freaking out because the 911 operator answered, and then put her on hold, only to come back to the call to say she was transferring her. I remember Mariah saying how ridiculous it was to be put on hold on a 911 call. Again, what seemed like forever to Mariah was likely just a few moments.

Luckily, there was an ambulance in our area so we didn't have to wait very long for the paramedics to arrive. By the time they got into the house, Jordan was already coming out of his seizure. He was in a daze, very confused and wondered why these strange people he didn't know were standing over him. Jordan had never experienced a seizure before so it was very confusing for him and very scary for Mariah and me. The paramedics checked Jordan over, asked him some basic questions and then transferred him onto a stretcher and into the ambulance.

After Mariah got off the phone with 911 her next call was to her Dad to ask him to come home right away. He was also close by and arrived home before Jordan was loaded into the ambulance. My husband, Mariah and I drove to meet the ambulance at the hospital, which was only a short drive from our home. It took about fifteen minutes before they would let us go into Emergency to see Jordan, but once they did, we saw that he was fine. He was tired but talking and joking with the nurses.

They kept him in the Emergency Department for the next several hours. At some point during the evening, as Jordan was quietly resting, I happened to check my phone. There was a message from a couple hours earlier that Ashley had left me. Apparently, Trevor had seen the ambulance pull up to our house and just kept saying over and over: "Please don't let that be for Jordan" "please don't let it be for Jordan." I guess Trevor was fine if Jim, Mariah or I were headed to the hospital as long as it was not his buddy Jordan. Then when Trevor saw it actually was Jordan being loaded into the ambulance Ashley said he went into hysterics thinking something awful had happened to Jordan. I felt terrible I hadn't received the message in time to call her back before they all went to bed but checking my phone earlier was the furthest thing from my mind. I sent her a text so she would see it as soon as they got up in the morning letting her know what was going on.

The doctors ran several tests to try and determine what may have caused Jordan's seizure. Nothing was conclusive. They decided to go ahead and send Jordan home later that same night. We were told that approximately one in ten people experience a seizure at one point or another in their lifetime. The doctor said: "It may never happen again, and if it doesn't, we may never learn the cause." We hoped, that would be the case for Jordan, that it was a one time occurrence. Unfortunately, we soon learned it wasn't. The next day, when I spoke to Ashley I apologized to her for not calling her back the night before. She completely understood. Then she told me how Trevor had cried himself to sleep with worry. I felt terrible for the poor little guy. Jordan made a point to visit with Trevor after school the next day so he could see for himself Jordan was okay. Earlier that day I had taken Jordan to be fitted with a heart monitor. The order for this had come from the emergency room doctor that was attending to Jordan the night before. He wanted Jordan to wear the heart monitor for the next two weeks, day and night. He was only allowed to take it off to shower. During the two weeks Jordan experienced several more mini seizures but nothing like the first one he had had.

More doctors, more tests and one more big seizure before we finally got a diagnosis that Jordan had epilepsy. Seriously! Like he didn't already have enough on his plate! Jordan now had a neurologist to add to the list of doctors that would be overseeing his care. The neurologist put him on an anti-convulsive medication that he will need to take twice a day for the rest of his life (if he wants to drive that is). Try telling a seventeen year old they have epilepsy and, due to the medication they are on, they can't drink any alcohol. Jordan hadn't even had his first legal beer and now he was being told, that can't happen. He was a little perturbed to say the least.

Jordan also had to give up driving for approximately eight months. The first two months or so was while the doctors were figuring all this out. Then after his epilepsy diagnosis he was required to be on his medication and be seizure free for six months before he was allowed to drive again. Jordan hated giving up his license but he understood why it was necessary and how important it was that he comply, so he did. In the end, the Neurologist had selected the right drug for Jordan because thankfully, his seizures have never returned.

PART FOUR

The Road Ahead

CHAPTER 18

One More Surgery

With the identification hurdles all behind Jordan, he still had one more surgery on his mind. While not all transgender people desire surgery to change their genitals, some, like my son Jordan, feel that their transition is not fully complete without it. This surgery is commonly referred to as "bottom surgery". Bottom surgery can be any surgery that alters a person's genitalia. Changing genitalia from female to male is one of the surgeries that falls in the category of sex reassignment surgery.

In Ontario, sex reassignment surgery (SRS) can be covered by the Ontario Health Insurance Plan (OHIP) if the person meets the requirements. These include, among other things, having experienced life as the other gender and being on hormone therapy for at least one year as well as having referrals from a doctor at the CAMH gender identity clinic in Toronto.

In order to get in to see a doctor at the gender identity clinic at CAMH, a person needs to be referred to them by their doctor. Jordan's doctor made this referral for him but so far all we have received is a letter from CAMH saying they received the referral and they have placed Jordan on a waiting list. This waiting list is just to see a CAMH doctor for an initial consultation. The letter told us that it could take up to a year and a half before we would be called with an appointment date.

As I disclosed earlier, the youth division of the CAMH gender identity clinic has closed. This has not affected Jordan because, while he was placed on their wait list prior to this closure, he has since turned eighteen and can be seen by the adult gender identity clinic. For now, we remain on the waiting list. It has already been thirteen months at the time of this writing.

Once Jordan gets his appointment, it could take some time before the CAMH doctors write their recommendation for surgery to OHIP. After OHIP receives the recommendation for coverage from CAMH, it could be another couple of months before they notify Jordan of their decision and outline what coverage he is entitled to. It is only after Jordan has a letter from OHIP saying they will cover his surgery that he can contact the surgeon and get on his waiting list. You can see why this whole process could take years.

While my husband and I were reluctant to go the CAMH route initially we see no reason for concern at this stage. Jordan has been living successfully as his authentic self now for approximately five years and it is our expectation that once he does get in to see the doctors at CAMH there should be little or no hesitation in writing him a recommendation for surgery.

In November of 2015 the provincial government announced that it wanted to change the policy so that the referral to OHIP for SRS could come from any qualified doctor in the province, not only a CAMH doctor. This policy change took until March of 2016 to come through. Prior to that OHIP would only accept a recommendation if it came from CAMH. The reality is that CAMH has become a bottleneck for people most in need of the surgery. There are simply too many people in need and too little medical staff available at CAMH to serve them.

With the guidelines changed in Ontario, people can now seek referral to OHIP from their individual doctor. This should speed things up. The bottleneck for access to the CAMH gender identity clinic should also begin to clear. However, even though this policy change means less wait time to get to the approval stage from OHIP, one large problem still exists. The problem is that there are not enough surgeons trained on sex reassignment surgeries to fill the need. This translates into long wait times for the surgeries, sometimes two years or more. At the time of this writing, OHIP doesn't even have an approved surgeon in the province of Ontario to send patients to.

OHIP is currently referring sex reassignment surgeries out of province to a surgeon in Quebec. The surgeon, located in Montreal, is Dr. Pierre Brassard. He has patients travel not only from Ontario, but from all across Canada, throughout the United States and from overseas to his clinic in Montreal. He has the experience and the facilities that make him a desirable choice as a sex reassignment surgeon.

At his Montreal practice, Dr. Brassard's team performs both top (chest) and bottom (genital) surgeries as well as other cosmetic procedures. A patient is required to arrive one to two days prior to surgery and will stay up to two weeks following their procedures. Only the first two or three days are spent at the actual clinic where the surgery is performed before the patient is transferred to a neighbouring property for recovery. The recovery house is fully staffed with around the clock nursing care and provides a safe and secure place for the patient to recuperate. Should a patient be pre-approved through OHIP, it is my understanding the health care plan will pay for not only the actual surgery but for the aftercare as well. What I understand not to be covered is the patient's travel to and from Montreal and any necessary accommodations for a family member who may be accompanying them. Dr. Brassard's team performs two hundred sex reassignment surgeries per year.

According to Dr. Brassard's own website before he will perform any surgery, the patient must first pass the following tests: An HIV test, Urine analysis, blood sugar, blood urea nitrogen, CBC (complete blood count) and, if over the age of forty, a Resting E.K.G. with interpretation.

The two procedure options available for female to male patients like Jordan looking for bottom surgery are either a metoidioplasty or a phalloplasty. A metoidioplasty is the simpler of the two surgeries, costs less, has fewer potential complications and takes about 2-3 hours to complete. With a metoidioplasty, the surgeon uses existing female genitalia to form a penis.

Phalloplasty, unlike the metoidioplasty procedure uses tissue from either the patient's arm or leg to build out a neopenis. This means the patient actually has two surgical sites that will need to recover. There could possibly be even a third site if a skin graft is needed. The phalloplasty surgery takes upwards of 8-10 hours to complete, costs far more and has the potential for more complications. The phalloplasty is often followed up by a second surgery to have an erectile prosthesis implanted along with testicular implants. Following recovery, phalloplasty patients are more likely to be capable of sexual penetration due to the larger size of the penis, but usually experience a lesser degree of sensation.

In both cases, standing to pee is possible following a successful surgery. I will not go into further detail here as it is best to consult with a surgeon directly in order to fully understand the different procedures, their possible complications and what's best for the individual. Jordan, who has since turned eighteen, believes he knows which of the two surgeries is right for him. At the time of this writing, we are still awaiting funding approval from OHIP. We have not booked an appointment with the surgeon, although I have been advised by his secretary that there is an approximate twenty month long wait list. This gives Jordan plenty of time to finalize his decision.

CHAPTER 19

The Dating Game

Dating can be complicated enough, but mix in being transgender and complicated goes to a whole new level. I hope we can all agree that everyone is deserving of romantic love and that there is no exception for a transgender person. Love can elude the best of us for the most fickle reasons, let alone, the more complicated ones. Dating is like a rite of passage; a time of self discovery. It is often when we ascertain as much about ourselves as we do about the person we are dating. We discover what is truly important to us in a partner. We learn what attributes we value most, and when we fall short of our 'ideal' person, what attributes we are willing to forgo. If all goes well, and we are lucky enough, we may just find 'the one'.

Some transgender people may feel they have a unique perspective of gender, making them more understanding and compassionate in relationships. I am not sure Jordan would feel that way given he has always had such a strong male self image but I have never asked him.

When to disclose is an important consideration for any transgender person and their personal safety should always be a consideration prior to disclosure. Being safe when dating is not just something for transgender people to think about, although they can be more vulnerable to unsuspected violence than cisgender people. Finding a way to gauge whether the person you are dating or considering dating is knowledgeable and accepting of transgender people is prudent. Often discussing any LGBT topic will give you an opportunity to measure their reaction and determine whether or not they are likely to be sensitive to transgender people in general. If these conversations are in person rather than on the phone or online, there is the added advantage of being able to observe their body language. Depending on the situation, a direct approach might make more sense. Asking them: "Do you know what a transgender person is?" can be a good starter. This is the approach Jordan used when he came out to members of our extended family. By asking them directly the insight garnered by their response should provide some direction on how best to approach the conversation from there.

Jordan had a couple of girlfriends in high school and both of them were very accepting of his past. In both cases they were friends first and Jordan disclosed only when the topic of dating became serious. We can only hope, that now that their dating relationships have come to an end, these young ladies will not share the information they know about Jordan with others.

There is also an argument to be made for whether disclosure

is necessary at all. Once SRS (sex reassignment surgery) has been completed it is possible, even under the most intimate of circumstances, that a transgender person could be presumed to be a cisgender person. If the transgender person has had SRS and is living fully in their desired gender they may want to leave the past in the past. Some transgender people prefer to use the term gender-affirming surgery to SRS, because for them it more accurately represents how they feel about these procedures. Once complete, they may look at their own SRS or gender-affirming surgery as nothing more than a piece of their medical history. For emotional health reasons, distancing themselves from their past and not thinking of themselves pre-surgery might actually be what is best for them.

Why should it be expected that SRS be disclosed at all? What if the medical history we were discussing was a kidney transplant? That would not likely be expected to be disclosed when dating. I recognize that sex reassignment surgery, or gender-affirming surgery, is very different from a kidney transplant. I am only trying to express how they are both private pieces of one's medical history.

One of the outcomes following SRS is an inability to have biological children (this excludes situations where pre-surgery measures have been taken; like the freezing of eggs or sperm for example). Could a person's inability to have children be disclosed to someone without having to reveal the person's gender history?

Perhaps, perhaps not.

My perspective, as the mother of a transgender person, is naturally my concern for my child. However, it is only fair that we try to see it from the perspective of the other person in the relationship. Depending on the individual, a transgender history could be a monumental thing or it could be insignificant. Regardless, if building a long term relationship is the goal, then I think disclosure to the other person is fair, honest and respectful.

If the transgender person is out publicly then there is a greater chance this conversation goes more smoothly, but seriously, what do I know? I sure don't have the answers and doubt you do either. I can only devise it would be more difficult for someone like my son who is living a stealth life because it is highly unlikely the other person has any inkling. If one discloses too soon and the relationship goes nowhere, there is now another person out there holding your secret. The more people that know, the more vulnerable that person may feel. Conversely, waiting too long to disclose could leave the other person feeling betrayed or jilted in some way. I imagine striking the right balance might be challenging.

There is a lot to reflect on when it comes to dating. As an ally we must trust the transgender people in our lives to figure this out for themselves. Sharing uninvited opinions like, "you need to tell them now" or, "if you don't disclose, you will ruin things before they start" aren't helpful and only add pressure to the situation. Just like each person is different, so is each relationship and navigating that is something only the ones in the situation can do, so I say unless we are asked for our opinion, we butt out.

One thing I can say for sure is that when someone accepts and loves someone else for exactly who they are, it is a beautiful thing.

CHAPTER 20

Looking to The Future

When my children were young, I always told them they can be anything and do anything they want in life. It was important to me that they felt empowered, deserving and self confident. I believe that young children will believe what we tell them. I believe if we feed their psyche with positive life affirming thoughts, they are much more likely to have a positive life experience. I took it to be my job as a parent to build up my children and do my best to speak life over them with my words and actions. Jim would do the same. He would always say to them: “It doesn’t matter what you choose to do in life, just as long as you do it well and you enjoy it.”

So, we as parents were prepared to support our children in whatever they wanted to do. I just never thought in a million years that one of my children would want to become the opposite gender. It has been an interesting journey but not an easy one. Through it all, I admired my son’s strength, courage and his conviction.

The comparison between Jordan pre-transition and Jordan today is remarkable. Besides the obvious physical differences, there have been clear changes in his emotional health and personality. The two years before transition when his outward expression was female, he was quiet and lacked confidence. He appeared detached from life and was unmotivated to change that. Withdrawn and depressed is the best way I can describe how he seemed. He had become an introvert. This was very different from the outgoing gregarious personality he had as a young child. After transition, his outgoing personality returned. He laughs louder, smiles often and aspired to be stronger both emotionally and physically. I see jubilation now when I look at Jordan. There is a sense of peace and contentment about him that was not there before. I see his bright smile and know that, today, he is more present and happier than he has ever been. He now exudes confidence and happiness from a place where darkness and despair used to be.

I realize that while some people strongly disagree with how we handled Jordan's situation, I don't need to let that fact affect me. I gave birth to two remarkable human beings. In doing so I, along with their father, took on the responsibility to nurture, guide and raise them to the best of our ability. That is exactly what Jim and I have done. If we try to parent our children and try to keep everyone happy at the same time, we can't do our job. At least, I don't see how we can. Parenting may just be the toughest job in the world, but I can attest that it is also truly rewarding.

Jim and I have been judged by some for moving too fast with

Jordan. Others, I am sure feel we did not act swiftly enough. Outside contrarian or negative influences can be valuable; but only if we use them for information and education. Otherwise, it's just noise. At some point along this journey, I learned to turn down the noise and focus inward. After all, I'm not here to please everyone. If I were, I would be a politician. Once I learned to turn down the noise, I had a much stronger sense of everything. My priorities have never wavered. They have always been, and will continue to be, my family's health, their wellbeing and their happiness. Today, if the negative noise from others, about decisions we made regarding Jordan, ever starts to annoy me, I only have to look to Jordan. When I see his smiling face and look at the light in his eyes, that noise fades away.

Jim and I want our children to love themselves so that they, in turn, can share their love with others. Self-love is challenging for many people. It takes support, encouragement and perseverance to raise healthy self-loving children. Fortunately, we are up for the task.

Admittedly, these last few years have served to educate me to a point where knowledge has replaced ignorance. By using the word *ignorance*, I am not suggesting I was stupid or mean spirited, only that I was uneducated on what it truly means to be a transgender person. It is unfortunate that I did not seek to avail myself of such education before it involved a family member. Had I done so, I might have been able to recognize the signs Jordan was showing us. Jim and I certainly are not perfect parents, but through trial and error, we have managed to deliver both Mariah and Jordan to adulthood. Each one of them is stronger for the experiences they have had and battles they have fought.

My greatest fear, even now, is that Jordan will somehow fall victim to some homophobic, trans hating, agenda pushing, closed minded idiot. Wow, that sounded a bit harsh! Unfortunately, some people are that harsh. They have little to zero understanding of, or any desire to understand, what it means to be transgender person. Those people scare me. The news and media have definitely provoked this fear in me and done little to help to reduce my anxiety. Meanwhile, my son goes about his day to day routine seemingly oblivious to the possibility of any such danger, or so it seems to me anyway. Early on, I had nightmares about him meeting some ugly fate that literally scared me awake at night. Thankfully, with each month and year that passes, Jordan settles more and more into living the stealth life he desires and my fears and anxieties abate. Though, if you are a parent, you will understand when I tell you my fear will never be gone completely.

I would like to share with you a recurring dream I had during my pregnancy with Jordan which, in hindsight, I find quite interesting now. It was a strange dream. In the dream I stood around a conveyer belt with dozens of other new moms. We were lined up around this conveyer belt, just standing there waiting for our babies to come around the belt and stop in front of us. Looking down the belt, I saw each baby wrapped up tightly in a blanket, either a blue blanket for the boys or a pink blanket for the girls. In my dream, each time the belt would stop in front of me I would look down at my baby and the blanket would be a different colour than the last time I had the dream. But that wasn't even the strange part. The strange part was that every time I unwrapped my baby, the physical did not match what the blanket suggested. So, if the blanket was pink I would unwrap my baby to discover a baby boy. If the blanket was blue, I would unwrap my baby and discover a baby girl. It was as if this dream was somehow preparing me that we don't always get what we expect. Luckily, while I may have had my expectations regarding gender, all I really wanted was another healthy baby, and that is exactly what I received.

Along my parenting journey I have reflected back on how I was raised by my own parents. I was not raised to hate anyone or to believe I was any better than anyone else. My siblings and I were taught to respect others regardless of whether we agreed with them or their life choices. We were led by examples of compassion, kindness and love. My husband and I have tried to instil these same values in our children and have led them through our own examples. When Mariah and Jordan were quite young, we had conversations with them about how they would come into contact with many different types of people over the course of their lives. We talked about the multicultural world we live in and that they should embrace that, even celebrate it. We told them if they are always tolerant and respectful of others, it would go a long way to ensuring their success in life. It seems our words did not fall on deaf ears because both Mariah and Jordan have grown up to be kind, respectful and compassionate individuals.

I can recall the primary school my children attended and how it celebrated the diversity of their student population. A welcoming hello to visitors covered the walls in the main lobby of the school. Not just a hello in English, but in every language spoken by their students. Each greeting proudly displayed on brightly coloured paper. What a great way to demonstrate community and togetherness and a fine example to set for the young students in their school.

When it comes time to leave this earth, we will all leave a legacy behind. I hope the one my family leaves will speak positively to the kind of people we were, how we made others feel and the impact knowing us had on their lives. At the end of the day, how we treat others, I believe, is what defines us most and what truly matters.

Today, Jordan is eighteen and just a few weeks away from graduating high school. He is giving serious thought to future studies in psychology and possibly even medical school. His life experiences give him empathy and understanding towards others. This, along with his caring personality, I believe makes him well suited to either endeavour. Regardless of where his life takes him from here, his future looks very bright.

Mariah, now in her twenties, has a job that she really enjoys and is living on her own. We get together for regular family dinners and she visits home multiple times a week. I feel very close to her and no longer worry about the impact others have on her. She has come full circle and returned to the loving big sister she was from the start. She caringly refers to Jordan as her brother and has accepted the change in both him and our family.

My two children are good friends again, communicating and partaking in each others lives. The love and laughter between them has returned and, for the first time in a long time, I see my family as whole once again. And for that, I am so very thankful.

CHAPTER 21

Some Final Thoughts

An important note about pronouns: It is always important to use the appropriate pronoun when addressing a transgender person. In order to be respectful, only the pronoun that aligns with their gender identity should be used. In most cases, this is also the pronoun that aligns with their gender expression. If you are still unsure, the best advice I can give you is to listen. Often, others close to the person are already using the appropriate pronoun and you can just listen and follow their lead. In the event you do make a mistake, just apologize, correct and quickly move on. Drawing too much attention to the error may only cause more discomfort for the transgender person and others.

In the beginning of my story, I used female pronouns to describe my son. I meant no disrespect to him or any other transgender person reading this story. I was speaking from my perspective at the time and, at that time, Jordan was my daughter. Today, if I talk about Jordan as a young child or even as a baby I refer to him only with male pronouns. Based on the timing of the story, and the way it unfolded, I used the pronouns I felt were appropriate.

I also tried to be respectful with the terms I chose to use in describing transgender people. I have become aware that some transgender people are offended by the term transgenders or the abbreviated term trans, and some are not. I also learned that some non-transgender people are offended by the term cisgender. It is possible, that my choice of terminology, in one place or another, throughout this book may have offended someone. Please know there was no intent to be disrespectful. I have come to the conclusion that it is virtually impossible to write in a way that everyone would be satisfied. Hopefully, it is the story itself that has resonated most with you regardless of the gender terms or pronouns I chose to use.

You should always use a transgender person's chosen name when addressing them, or speaking to others about them. Insisting on using their given name or birth name is not only disrespectful but inconsiderate and hurtful. You should honour them by using their chosen name regardless of whether or not it has been made legal.

Please be careful not to out a transgender person. If they are not disclosing the fact they are a transgender person to others you certainly should not be disclosing it. If you have this information about someone, please understand this information is private and very personal. It could be considered to be medical information. As such, it deserves the same level of privacy we would assign any other piece of a person's medical information. Sharing this information would be an invasion of privacy and could have very negative consequences. Even if you think the person you want to tell would never share, or in your opinion, has some right to know, it's not your place to tell them. Not everyone is accepting and tolerant and outing a transgender person could result in job loss, social out casting, damaged relationships and even physical harm.

What I can tell you is that if a transgender person, who is not out to the world, comes out to you personally, it speaks volumes about the level of faith they have in you. Their decision to discuss their transgenderism with you gives you a very intimate look into who they are. It is a display of both honour and trust that they choose to share this with you.

When I think about the transgender person who has to think about their surroundings and their personal safety on a regular basis, it must be wearying. I imagine thoughts that should be reserved for productive day to day activities are often swallowed up and replaced with discriminatory distractions that lead to worry and even fear. What a terrible way to live.

I dislike that we live at a time when there is so much controversy around gender. There is so much misinformation and prejudice out there. I get that society would like to have everyone fit nicely into a pink or blue box, but that is just not realistic. In addition to transgender people like my son Jordan, there are other people who do not see their mental gender as opposite to their biological sex yet they still consider themselves to be a transgender person. I do not want to confuse or digress too much here. Having said that, I will offer you one example. Someone who considers themselves to be a gender fluid individual may refer to themselves as a transgender person or even as a genderqueer person. Gender fluid individuals do not see themselves as just one gender. They flow between the binary definitions of male and female and are very comfortable in doing so. Bottom line is that there is far more to gender than most people realize. A little education and a willingness to listen would go a long way towards bridging the gap on both sides of this, for some reason, still contentious subject.

So many transgender people have wonderful stories to share that can be of great value to others but often those stories never get told for fear of being exposed. I hope that publishing this book was not a mistake and that it resonates with those who need it most. If it can help even one transgender person or one family to find peace then it has been a success, in my opinion.

The best way to interact with a transgender person is the same way you would interact with any other human being. Love them for whom they are, honour them and respect them because everyone has the right to live their life as their authentic self. If you or someone you love needs courage due to a gender struggle, I hope that strength is there when it is needed most. Every person deserves to be comfortable with their own gender.

While looking through old photos can be an enjoyable pastime for some of us, for a transgender person it can be uncomfortable, even painful. It may dredge up old feelings that they would prefer to leave buried. Jordan prefers not to look at pictures of himself before his transition. To be more accurate, he does not like to look at pictures that do not line up with his male gender identity. Out of respect for Jordan, any pictures depicting him as a girl have been removed from sight. This includes all those wonderful glamour shot photos I received back when he was only four. After all that effort and money spent, today, those glamour pictures of Jordan are hidden away in the bottom of a box somewhere. Fortunately for us, we do have many pictures of a younger Jordan that we are able to display and share. This is because back when he was younger his gender expression was male, even though we had not yet recognized him as being transgender.

Transgender people make up a very small percentage of the population. Many statistics show they make up only 0.5% of the total population in North America. However, with so many transgender people like my son Jordan choosing to live stealth lives getting an accurate percentage is difficult, if not impossible. If some of these people decide to have surgery then there is a greater chance they are included in the estimated percentage.

With society's poor treatment of transgender people it is no wonder so many prefer to live surreptitiously. It is possible you have already been interacting with a transgender person without even knowing it. They could be your next door neighbour, your taxi driver, the cashier where you shop for groceries, even a close family friend. Ask yourself, if someone you have been interacting with on a regular basis came out to you as transgender, would you somehow feel different about them? Would you begin to treat them any differently? Believing that you would is a very real fear many transgender people have. They are living their life, just like you and me, trying to have the best human experience they can in the time they are here.

It is understandable that you may be curious about certain behaviours of transgender people, but understand your curiosity doesn't make it your business. Nor does it give you the right to ask them anything you want. You would likely find it offensive if someone asked you about your genitals. So, don't ask a transgender person about theirs. What surgeries they have or haven't had, what washroom they use, how they have sex are all questions that should never be asked. They are all private matters.

I often wonder how different our lives would be if out of all our human traits, love was the most prevalent. If it were, love should easily trump gender discrimination. Yet, sadly, it has not. There is no question there is still discrimination and bigotry out there and not just towards the transgender community. With over six billion people on the planet, eliminating it all seems insurmountable. I think we need to make a decision as to whether or not, we as individuals, are going to fuel that fire or help to extinguish it.

It will not be until love overcomes discrimination that we will discover peace in this world. For now, there is something you and I can do. We can express compassion, understanding and basic human kindness towards others regardless of things like race, gender and sexual orientation. Hopefully, the rest of the world will eventually catch up. I, for one, just wish the rest of the world would start pedaling a little faster.

I agonized for quite a while on whether on not publishing this book was a good idea. If it was going to be published, it was important that I find a way that would not out my son. I want to help others to understand they are not alone and that there are other families who may bc going through what they are going through. I wanted others to benefit from our experiences but at the same time I needed to ensure my son was safe and his identity protected. For this reason I ask any of our close friends and family members reading this book that you respect Jordan and his desire to live his life privately. If you enjoyed our story and want to share it with others you think could benefit, I ask that you do so without referencing our family or outing me as the author.

Much of what I have written about is undeniably controversial and I expect my opinions and views may ruffle a few feathers. I am okay with that. What is important is that by sharing this story we can open a dialog. We can start a conversation and get others thinking about the real people that make up the transgender community, rather than be blinded by the media's often tilted views. This story may even help someone who is struggling with, or questioning, their own gender identity to know they are not alone.

Societal pressures today are unlike anything we have seen in the past. We live in the social media and instant news age where hate can be disseminated around the globe in a matter of seconds. We should all try to remember that each of us has our own struggles and demands. Granted some are bigger than others, but we are all in this together. We are individuals living among a very diverse population challenged by politics, religion, political correctness, and much more. This challenges us to take a long hard look at ourselves and decide what it is we are going to stand for. Right wingers and left wingers continually battle hard to rally support for their positions. Minorities like the transgender community often get trampled on in the process. Some see society's recent liberations as just and long overdue. Others see us as a society on the precipice of moral chaos. I am not sure how we can find a comfortable middle ground everyone can live with. Opinions will always differ. There is no question about that. There will always be debates worthy of debating. If there weren't, it would make for a pretty boring world out there.

The thing about minorities is that it is too easy to ignore them. The sheer fact they are minorities suggests they should have little impact or influence on the majority. Today, as their voices get stronger we find that their influence is spreading and becoming overwhelmingly difficult to ignore. This is a good thing. While the majorities often try to disregard the societal contributions the minorities consistently put forth, it does not diminish the value of what they have to say. We should be listening more with open minds and open hearts. We should recognize how difficult it must be for them to push against the barriers erected by the strong majorities. If we can set aside our own feelings long enough to listen we may just be surprised by what we hear. We have stepped on minorities long enough. It is time to exercise our heart muscles and verify not only the existence of minorities like the transgender community, but acknowledge they deserve the same rights and freedoms we do. One thing always stays true; the clear fact that each of us is human and we are all deserving of the same civil rights and liberties.

"The greatness of humanity is not in being human, but in being humane"
~ Gandhi

Finally, I would like to share some of my family's final thoughts with you. My husband Jim was the first person I shared my writing with. Up until that point, nobody was even aware I was documenting our journey. It was around the time I began to consider this might be something worth publishing that I decided to share it with him. His initial read of the manuscript was an emotional one. He encouraged me to finish it and acted as my personal sounding board whenever I needed one.

After sharing it with Jim and getting a little further along with the story I invited Jordan to take a look. Jordan's unexpectedly strong reaction to some of my writing surprised me. He honestly did not get very far before confronting me about some of the verbiage I had chosen to use. Specifically, he was angry at the fact I mentioned that we had to mourn our daughter. The word 'mourn' struck a chord with Jordan and he didn't understand why I would use that word. He said, and quite sternly I might add, "I didn't die. I am still here." At that moment a wave of guilt swept over me. I felt guilty for the way I expressed what was in my heart. Should I have found another way to express what I was feeling? Did saying I had to mourn my daughter make me a bad mother? It is true that mourn is usually a word we reserve when someone has died, but it did seem to fit how I was feeling. Perhaps 'sorrow' would have been a better word to use, but it was too late now. Jordan just sat there waiting for my response.

What I tried to convey to my son was that while he obviously had not died, the part of him, that part that I knew as my daughter, was in fact gone. I would never again hear that feminine voice that testosterone took away. Even though Jordan's gender expression was male for all but two years of his life, I still thought of him as my daughter back then. Sometimes, I think it would have been nice if I had of thought to record his voice prior to his transition. It might be neat to have that, though again, I don't think Jordan would agree with me.

He also took issue with my concern for what God thought. Perhaps he worried about the amount of emphasis I placed on this in my writing. It is an important topic because religion and church so strongly influence attitudes. Along with that influence there is great responsibility, not unlike the responsibility parents have for their children. Jordan asked me point blank: "Why did you care so much about what God thought anyway?" I explained that for our sakes, as much as for his own, we needed to do our due diligence and look at many things before deciding on a course of action. My curiosity about what God thought was just one of those things. Regardless of the answers I found when I asked the question "What does God think?" I told Jordan that I knew in my heart it would not deter me from doing what I felt was best for him.

I can not negate the fact that had Mariah not been resisting the idea of Jordan's transition as much as she was, I may not have explored the topic quite as deeply as I did. When I looked for what was at the root of society's rejection of transgender people, I saw the Bible in many instances. This was what drove me to read it, in its entirety, for myself. The goal was not just to educate myself but to try to understand where others were coming from. I wanted to help Mariah, as well as any future readers of this story, who may be struggling to come to terms with a loved one who is transgender. For this reason, a chapter that was quite short grew larger in reaction to the struggle I witnessed within my daughter.

I also explained to Jordan that while he was certain, he wanted to transition from the beginning, his father and I worried he may have regrets later on. He said: "It was my decision. You only needed to consent. If I regret anything, which I won't, I would not blame you." I appreciate that Jordan says he would not blame us, but the thing is that Jim and I *would* blame ourselves and that is exactly what I told Jordan.

When children are older, over the age of eighteen, we have less control. We can continue to offer guidance and support though, ultimately, it is they themselves that will be responsible for their outcomes, their victories, and their regrets. At the time, Jordan was still a minor and, our consent was required.

After Jordan's review, I also changed a chapter heading. Chapter two was originally titled "Teachers & Strangers - Fooled Another One" and it became simply "Teachers & Strangers." I decided to make the change because Jordan felt strongly, that while it may have been the way I saw those stories, he was not intentionally fooling anyone. He felt the chapter heading was misleading. He explained to me that he was never trying to purposely fool anyone and there was no malice on his part whatsoever. He was just being who he was. It was the teachers and strangers that fooled themselves through the assumptions they made about his gender.

Jordan is intelligent enough to understand that the vulnerabilities I expressed in my writing, while a reflection on me do not at all diminish my commitment to him or my devotion to our family. Nothing can diminish the fact that I am over the moon grateful he is here and is finally happy with whom he is. Having Jordan as our son is wonderful and we feel very blessed to have him in our lives. Jim and I feel equally grateful and blessed to have Mariah as our daughter.

Mariah also wanted to read the manuscript but it was a difficult read for her as well. She found herself more emotionally affected by it than she expected. As it turned out, neither of my children finished reading it through to the end. One day I hope they will change their minds and pick it up again. Until then, this deeply personal memoir will serve as a record of our family's journey, here for them, if and when they feel the desire to finish it.

CHAPTER 22

Thank You

I want to thank you from the bottom of my heart for picking up this book and coming along on this journey with me. I hope that through the pages of this book, I have helped you in some small way. Perhaps you are on a similar path, or perhaps you are just curious about the topic and wanted to read one mother's story. Either way, I thank you.

If you are on a similar path, I wish I could be there for you in person. If for no other reason than to sit alongside you and listen to your own story, to your child's story, but I can't because to do that would reveal my son's identity and "I promised not to tell."

What I can do is offer you a friendship beyond the pages of this book. I have set up an email account for the sole purpose of communicating with you. That email address is writtenbymom@gmail.com and I promise to make a conscious effort to respond to your emails as quickly as possible. We all need someone to talk to and not everyone can understand the journey a family goes through in helping a loved one who has come out as transgender. Each family's journey is unique. I can't promise to have all the answers, but I will openly share any resources or advice I have that may make your own journey just a little bit easier. I wish you and your family happiness and hope that the path before you is always travelled with others who bring you love, support and peace.

I would like to end by sharing a quote with you that I hope will inspire anyone struggling with their gender identity. The author is unknown to me. "Be bold enough to use your voice. Brave enough to listen to your heart & strong enough to live the life you've always imagined."

Sincerely,

Cheryl B. Evans

P.S. If you enjoyed this book please give it a positive review. Positive reviews will encourage more people to read it. That way we can help educate others on what it truly means to be a transgender person and hopefully help to change society's perceptions. xo

Helpful Resources

I would like to share some valuable transgender resources that may help you along your own journey. The list below includes general reference websites, websites for FTM supplies like binders and packers and even a couple referral links to SRS surgeons.

Center of Excellence for Transgender health:
www.transhealth.ucsf.edu
Trans Family: www.transfamily.org
Mermaids: www.mermaidsuk.org.uk
Transforming Family: www.transformingfamily.org
Gender Spectrum: www.genderspectrum.org
National Center for Transgender equality: www.transequality.org
FTM International: www.ftmi.org
GLAAD: www.glaad.org/transgender
Human Rights Campaign (HRC) U.S.A: www.hrc.org
Egale Canada Human Rights Trust: www.egale.ca
Rainbow Health Ontario: www.rainbowhealthontario.ca
The Trevor Project (provides crisis intervention and suicide prevention for LGBTQ Youth ages 13-24): www.thetrevorproject.org

The place we ordered chest binders from is called Underworks. Their website is:
www.underworks.com

The place we ordered FTM packers from is called Reel Magik. Prosthetic glue is also available through this site and it is referred to as silicone medical adhesive. Their website is: www.reelmagik.com

The doctor that preformed Jordan's top surgery was Dr. Hugh McLean at the McLean Clinic in Mississauga, Ontario. I can't say enough about the staff and service we received from this clinic, very professional and very friendly. Jordan's surgical results were fantastic! Although this is no guarantee other patients will have the same results, it is honest feedback on the results my son experienced. Dr. McLean is an experienced and skilled plastic surgeon and, in my opinion, a great choice for FTM top surgery.

The doctor that we are looking to have do Jordan's bottom surgery is Dr. Pierre Brassard from Montreal, Quebec. If you are looking for a surgical team that offers some of the world's most extensive SRS experience then you may want to consider Dr. Brassard. For more information on this surgeon you can visit: www.grsmontreal.com the official website for his Gender Reassignment Surgery Clinic.

Helpful Terms to Understand

Transgender is the term used for a person who identifies themselves with a gender that is different from the gender of the body they were born into. The term transgender, because it encompasses so many different types of gender identity, is often referred to as an umbrella term. Simply put, someone is transgender when they perceive their gender in their mind differently from the gender suggested by their biological sex. This term is sometimes shortened to "Trans" although some transgender people find this shortened term offensive.

Transgenderism is the adjective used to describe the gender identity conflict of a transgender person.

Transgender Man is an individual who identifies as a male even though they were assigned female at birth. This term is sometimes shortened to FTM which stands for Female to Male.

Transgender Woman is an individual who identifies as a female even though they were assigned male at birth. This term is sometimes shortened to MTF which stands for Male to Female.

Cisgender is a term used to describe an individual who has a gender identity that matches the gender they were assigned at birth and is comfortable (both in mind and body) living in that gender. The term cisgender is the same as saying a non-transgender person. The majority of the population falls under this category.

Gender Identity is a term used to describe an individual's own sense of their gender. It is the gender one feels or believes in their mind they are. This is not visible to others as it refers to how one internalizes their own gender.

Gender Expression is a term used to describe the way one outwardly expresses their gender. Their voice, mannerisms, dress, and behaviour are all ways through which one can express their gender.

Cross-Dresser is a term used to describe a person who enjoys wearing the clothes typically worn by their opposite gender. A cross-dresser is not a transgender person. This is because cross-dressers do not have the same disconnect between their gender identity and the gender assigned to them at birth, the way transgender people do. Cross-Dressers can be heterosexual men, possibly even married men. A cross-dresser does not necessarily wear clothes of the opposite gender all the time, and may do so only on occasion.

Sexual Orientation is a term used to describe an individual's sexual or romantic attraction to others. A person's attraction may be to members of the same or different sex. For example someone attracted only to persons of the opposite sex are considered to be heterosexual. Someone attracted to persons of the same sex usually identify as lesbian or gay and would be described as homosexuals. Persons who are attracted to both sexes are referred to as bisexual. In the case of a transgender man being only attracted to women, his sexual orientation would be considered heterosexual.

Intersex is a term used for a person born with a sexual anatomy and/or chromosome makeup that does not seem to match typical definitions for what male or female are. An intersexed person may have a combination of characteristics that could make determining sex at birth difficult. One example of an intersex person is someone born with both male and female reproductive organs.

Gender Dysphoria is the term used to describe a person whose gender identity does not line up with the gender they were assigned at birth. This is usually the actual medical diagnosis for a transgender person and usually must be given before a doctor will start an individual on Hormone Therapy. Untreated, a person with gender dysphoria could feel displaced or out of sync because of the sheer conflict between their physical and mental realities. This stress can lead to depression or even suicide.

Hormone Replacement Therapy is a term used to refer to the hormones an individual is taking that are not naturally produced by their body. This therapy is usually monitored by the doctor who is prescribing the actual hormones. In the example of a FTM, they would be taking testosterone (also referred to as "T") and in the example of a MTF, they would be taking estrogen. These hormone medications are often administered through injections, oral medication or external creams. All the available options should be explored with a doctor prior to deciding on a treatment path. Most doctors want to see that a person has lived a gender role experience for a minimum of one year before starting hormone treatment. The term Hormone Replacement Therapy is sometimes shortened to HRT or HT (Hormone Therapy) for short.

Gender Role Experience is a term describing a time when a person is fully living in and experiencing life as a person of the gender they are looking to transition to. Gender Role Experience is often something doctors look for before they will recommend hormone therapy and or gender reassignment surgeries. The term Gender Role Experience is sometimes shortened to GRE.

Transition is a term used to describe the time when an individual begins living in the gender with which they identify rather than continuing to live in the gender of their birth. When someone enters transition, their name and their gender expression are often the first changes they will make. A transition is complete when the individual decides it is complete. Medical intervention such as hormone medications and surgery may or may not be part of one's transition.

Sex Reassignment Surgery refers to the surgical procedures an individual may choose to undergo in order to change the body they have to better reflect their gender identity. The most common surgeries are often referred to as top and/or bottom surgeries. Top surgery can be breast augmentation or removal and bottom surgery could be any surgery that alters the person's genitals. There are many different surgery types and options for a transgender person and it is important to note that not everyone may need or want surgery as part of their overall transition. The term sex reassignment surgery is often shortened to the acronym SRS. Some people prefer to say gender-affirming surgery to SRS, noting it as a more accurate representation to how they feel about these procedures.

LGBT is an acronym for Lesbian, Gay, Bi-Sexual, & Transgender. This term is also seen lengthened to LGBTQ with the Q representing Questioning or Queer. This term is also sometimes seen with an 'I' which, when present, would represent Intersexed.

Questioning is a term that describes a person's self discovery process. They are working on discovering who they are and may not yet be certain with regards to their sexual orientation and/or their gender identity.

Genderqueer is a term that describes a person who has a gender identity that falls outside the binary definitions of male and female. An example of a queer individual is someone who refers to themselves as gender fluid. They often prefer non-gender specific pronouns such as "they" instead of "he" or "she".

The list above is far from complete. There are many other terms you may have encountered regarding the LGBTQ community. The internet is a valuable resource and can help educate you further on any terms which you did not find on the list above.

Acknowledgments

This book would never have made it this far without the ongoing encouragement of my husband. You mean the world to me. You have always supported me in all that I have set out to do and this book was no different. I am forever grateful for your love and friendship and can't imagine sharing this life with anyone else.

I owe a great gratitude to my parents for always standing by me. You continually support both me and my family. Mom and Dad, you have blessed us in so many different ways. You are my greatest teachers. Thank you for the incredible examples you have set as terrific parents and grandparents. Mom, the hours you spent pouring over the manuscript is so appreciated. Thank you for being my sounding board and my very first editor.

There are others whom I am unable to mention by name but I am sure they know who they are. They took great care to read the manuscript and offer invaluable support, suggestions and corrections. They acted as my confidants and my editors. Even though their lives were crazy busy, they some how found the time to offer me support and guidance on this project. Thank you for the faith you have shown in me and the kindness you always show towards our family.

Above all I want to thank my children. You are the greatest gifts in my life. You are part of my soul. You are my purpose and my joy. No words can ever express the amount of love I have for each of you. You are so completely unique and wonderful just the way you are. I know seeing this book out in the world is not easy. It exposes such a raw and intimate side of everything we have experienced as a family over the last few years. But, I also know you understand that sharing our story may help other families or struggling individuals to know they are not alone. Your blessing to publish this shows great strength and courage. Thank you both for making my world so rich with love and happiness. I love you!

About The Author

I have been happily married to my husband Jim for more than twenty-three years and consider him to be my rock, my pillar and my best friend. Together we have raised two wonderful children, Mariah and Jordan. As cheesy as it sounds, I truly do just want what is best for my children, and above all else I want them to be happy. If you have finished reading this book you have likely already formed an opinion of me, or at least have a sense of who I am.

It is never an easy task to write about oneself, so I decided to enlist the help of my good friend, Julianna. I asked Julianna how she would describe me and this is what she wrote: "You are someone whose shoes I would like to walk in some days. You are determined, and ambitious, frank, persistent and supportive. You love to laugh, drink flavoured coffee and eat chocolate. You enjoy movies and reading non-fiction books. Which, you read to better yourself or just for interest. You will stop at nothing to support your kids, husband and family. You provide support to friends when they call crying. You are an advisor to all. No matter what the situation is you always come out strong and smiling."

After I read what Julianna wrote about me, I just smiled, and said to her "I wanted that written on my tombstone." Of course,

I was only joking. It's far too lengthy for a tombstone, and I have no plans to depart this life anytime soon. It does work nicely on this page, though. This gave me a chance to share it with you and acknowledge Julianna at the same time. Unfortunately, because of my need to keep my real identity a mystery I have to refrain from sharing specific details about myself. Nevertheless, I believe Julianna did a wonderful job of summarizing the essence that is me, also known as, Cheryl B. Evans.

If you would like to get to know me better, or hear about what I'm up to these days, you can follow me on twitter @writtenbymom. You can also connect with me through my website at www.writtenbymom.ca

Other Books by This Author:

What Does God Think? Transgender People and The Bible

Wonderfully and Purposely Made: I Am Enough

My Parenting Journey with an LGBTQ+ Child: A Journal

My Parenting Journey with a Transgender Child: A Journal

I Love You Unconditionally: A Journal for LGBTQ Children & Teens

Made in the USA
Middletown, DE
15 April 2024

53022266R00128